BEYOND THE NUMBERS

ELEVATING SALES NEGOTIATION FROM
TRANSACTIONAL TO TRANSFORMATIONAL

Anirban Majumder

Chennai • Bangalore

CLEVER FOX PUBLISHING
Chennai, India

Published by CLEVER FOX PUBLISHING 2024
Copyright © Anirban Majumder 2024

All Rights Reserved.
ISBN: 978-93-56489-84-4

This book has been published with all reasonable efforts taken to make the material error-free after the consent of the author. No part of this book shall be used, reproduced in any manner whatsoever without written permission from the author, except in the case of brief quotations embodied in critical articles and reviews.

The Author of this book is solely responsible and liable for its content including but not limited to the views, representations, descriptions, statements, information, opinions and references ["Content"]. The Content of this book shall not constitute or be construed or deemed to reflect the opinion or expression of the Publisher or Editor. Neither the Publisher nor Editor endorse or approve the Content of this book or guarantee the reliability, accuracy or completeness of the Content published herein and do not make any representations or warranties of any kind, express or implied, including but not limited to the implied warranties of merchantability, fitness for a particular purpose. The Publisher and Editor shall not be liable whatsoever for any errors, omissions, whether such errors or omissions result from negligence, accident, or any other cause or claims for loss or damages of any kind, including without limitation, indirect or consequential loss or damage arising out of use, inability to use, or about the reliability, accuracy or sufficiency of the information contained in this book.

Dedication

'I want to dedicate this book to my parents

Late Srimati Jayasree Majumder and Late Sri Alok Majumder who used to be my constant source of inspiration'

CONTENTS

About The Author .... *viii*
Introduction .... *x*

Chpater 1: Sales Negotiation 1
- ❏ Defining Sales Negotiation 1
- ❏ The Role of Negotiation in the Sales Process 3
- ❏ The Common Misconception: "It's All About Price" 5

Chpater 2: Preparing For Sales Negotiation 8
- ❏ Researching Your Customer: The Foundation of Sales Success 8
- ❏ Setting Clear Objectives: The North Star of Sales Success 13
- ❏ Building Your Value Proposition: Crafting the Persuasive Heart of Sales 16
- ❏ Identifying Potential Challenges: Navigating the Roadblocks to Sales Success 20

Chpater 3: Building Rapport And Trust 25
- ❏ The Importance of Trust in Sales: The Cornerstone of Success 25

Contents

- Establishing Credibility: The Art of Trust and Expertise 30
- Effective Communication Techniques: The Art of Persuasion and Connection 34
- Building Long-Term Relationships: The Heartbeat of Sales Success 38

Chpater 4: Introduction To The Art Of Listening 43

- Active Listening Skills: The Catalyst for Connection and Understanding 43
- Asking Powerful Questions: The Key to Insight and Influence 48
- Uncovering Customer Needs and Pain Points: The Foundation of Effective Sales 52
- Demonstrating Empathy: The Bedrock of Customer-Centric Sales 56

Chpater 5: Negotiation Strategies 61

- Win-Win vs. Win-Lose Approaches: Shaping the Dynamics of Negotiation 62
- Principled Negotiation (Getting to Yes): The Art of Agreement 66
- The Power of BATNA: Unveiling Your Negotiation Safety Net 69
- Creating Value in Negotiation: The Art of Expanding the Pie 74

Chpater 6: Handling Objections And Pushback 80
- ❏ Identifying Common Objections in Sales: Anticipating and Overcoming Challenges 81
- ❏ Responding Effectively to Objections: Turning Challenges into Opportunities 86

Chpater 7: Price Negotiation 93
- ❏ Pricing Strategies: Beyond Numbers 94
- ❏ Defending Your Pricing 99
- ❏ Handling Price Objections 104
- ❏ Negotiating Discounts & Terms 109

Chpater 8: Closing The Deal 116
- ❏ Recognizing Buying Signals 116
- ❏ The Art of Closing Techniques 122
- ❏ Overcoming Final Hurdles 128
- ❏ Ensuring Smooth Transitions to Implementation 132

Chpater 9: Negotiating In Complex Sales 138
- ❏ Dealing with Multiple Stakeholders 138
- ❏ Navigating B2B Sales Negotiations 142
- ❏ Handling Competitive Bidding Scenarios 145
- ❏ Managing Long Sales Cycles 148

Chpater 10: Handling Difficult Situations 152
- ❏ Dealing with Aggressive Buyers 152
- ❏ Negotiating in a Stalemate 156
- ❏ Escalating to Higher Authority 158
- ❏ Resolving Deadlocks in a Negotiations 162

Chpater 11: Post Negotiation: Maintaining Customer Satisfaction 167
- ❑ Delivering on Promises: The Keystone of Customer Satisfaction 168
- ❑ Managing Expectations: The Art of Surpassing What's Promised 172
- ❑ Strategies to Avoid Post-Sale Disputes: Nurturing Smooth Sailing 176
- ❑ Building Customer Loyalty: The Art of Cultivating Unbreakable Bonds 180

Chpater 12: Continuous Improvement In Sales Negotiation 184
- ❑ The Role of Feedback in Sales Negotiation: Navigating Success 185
- ❑ Learning from Each Negotiation: Unveiling the Treasures Within 189
- ❑ Developing Your Negotiation Skills: Unveiling the Path to Excellence 194
- ❑ Staying Updated with Industry Trends: Navigating the Shifting Tides 198

Conclusion *202*
- ❑ A Journey to Mastery: Conclusion 202
- ❑ Recap of Key Takeaways 202
- ❑ Encouragement for Ongoing Improvement 203
- ❑ Parting Thought on Becoming a Masterful Sales Negotiator 204

ABOUT THE AUTHOR

*A*nirban stands as a beacon of dedication and passion in the world of business development. With an impressive tenure of 24 years, he has not only mastered the art of building high-performing sales teams but has also excelled in negotiating complex deals. His journey in sales, marketing, and negotiation is marked by a deep-rooted customer-centric approach, which has been the cornerstone of his success.

What sets Anirban apart is his unwavering motivation and result-driven ethos. He doesn't just aim for targets; he strives to exceed them, consistently pushing the boundaries of what's possible in sales and business growth. His experience spans various multinational companies, both in India and abroad, giving him a diverse and rich perspective on global business strategies.

Anirban's expertise in nurturing and leading sales teams is noteworthy. He doesn't just manage teams; he inspires them. Under his leadership, teams don't just function; they flourish, driven by the same passion and dedication that he embodies. His approach is not just about hitting numbers; it's about building relationships, understanding customer needs, and delivering value that goes beyond the conventional.

About The Author

In the complex world of deal-making, Anirban's negotiation skills shine the brightest. He has a knack for navigating through the intricacies of large-scale deals with ease and finesse. His negotiation style is a blend of empathy, strategic insight, and a deep understanding of market dynamics, making him a formidable presence in any business discussion.

Anirban's journey is not just a career; it's a testament to his relentless pursuit of excellence in the realms of sales, marketing, and negotiation. His experience and achievements make him not just a leader but a mentor and an inspiration to many in the industry.

INTRODUCTION

*I*n the world of sales, negotiation is the linchpin of success. It's the pivotal moment when the art of persuasion meets the science of strategy, and it's the difference between closing deals that catapult your career and watching opportunities slip through your fingers. Whether you're a seasoned sales professional seeking to refine your skills or a newcomer eager to master the craft, you hold in your hands a roadmap to negotiation mastery.

Welcome to Beyond the Numbers: Elevating Sales Negotiation from Transactional to Transformational. This book is your guide to navigating the intricate terrain of sales negotiations with confidence, finesse, and, most importantly, a track record of success. In the pages that follow, we will embark on a transformative journey together, one that will equip you with the tools, techniques, and insights needed to excel in the dynamic and competitive world of sales.

Negotiation is not a solitary endeavour; it's an intricate manufactured dialogue that carries a flow of emotions which will help you to connect with your customer with a mindset of exchanging values. It's about understanding your customers' needs, uncovering their motivations, and crafting agreements that benefit both parties. It's about building lasting relationships where trust and mutual respect are the cornerstones of every deal.

In this book, we will delve into the core principles of negotiation strategy, dissect the psychology of persuasion, and explore practical techniques that have been tested and proven in the field by sales professionals at the top of their game. Whether you're negotiating prices, terms, or contracts, the principles and tactics you'll learn here are versatile and adaptable to a wide range of scenarios.

But this book is more than a manual for deal-making; it's a resource for personal growth and professional development. Negotiation is not just about what you do; it's also about who you become. As you embrace the strategies within these pages, you'll find yourself not only closing more deals but also becoming a more confident, empathetic, and influential communicator.

Each chapter is designed to provide you with actionable insights and practical advice that you can immediately apply to your sales negotiations. From the art of active listening to the science of objection handling, from the nuances of pricing strategies to the psychology of closing deals, we will leave no stone unturned in our quest to elevate your negotiation prowess.

So, are you ready to embark on this transformative journey? Are you ready to unlock the secrets to sales negotiation success? If so, let's begin. Your path to becoming a masterful sales negotiator is about to start now.

CHAPTER 1

SALES NEGOTIATION

Defining Sales Negotiation

Sales Negotiation delves into the intricate tapestry of the sales world, where each thread represents a vital aspect of negotiation, a skill as ancient as commerce itself yet ever-evolving in its form and function. Sales negotiation is not just a business term; it's an art, a science, and a delicate exchange of human interaction, all woven into one dynamic process.

At its heart, sales negotiation is the process of reaching an agreement between two parties, each with their own unique set of desires and limitations. It's a conversation, a delicate balancing act between giving and taking. Imagine a vendor at a bustling market artfully engaging with a potential buyer. The vendor doesn't just sell a product; they sell an experience, an opportunity. This is sales negotiation in its purest form - an exchange of value where both parties seek a mutually beneficial outcome.

Take, for instance, the story of a small tech start-up negotiating with a giant corporation for a partnership. The start-up brings innovative ideas and agility, while the corporation offers scale and resources. The negotiation here is not just about numbers; it's a thrilling and exciting process and experience in which each one is learning and adapting to the other's strengths and weaknesses.

Sales negotiation is deeply rooted in psychology. It's about understanding not just what the other party wants but why they want it. Consider a real estate agent negotiating a house sale. They don't just sell a structure of bricks and mortar; they sell a dream, a future home. The agent listens, empathizes, and aligns their pitch to the emotional wavelengths of the buyers. This psychological insight is what turns a mere discussion about price into a meaningful conversation about value.

This process also thrives on strategy. Each negotiation is a chess game, requiring foresight, planning, and adaptability. Effective negotiators are like grandmasters, thinking several moves ahead. They understand the power of tactics like anchoring, where the first number put on the table sets the tone for the negotiation, or the rule of reciprocity, where a concession from one side leads to a concession from the other.

But sales negotiation is not just a game of tactics; it's also a journey of self-discovery and personal growth. It challenges individuals to be better listeners, more empathetic communicators, and more creative problem-solvers. It's a skill that transcends the boardroom, enriching personal relationships and everyday interactions.

Above all, sales negotiation is about building lasting relationships. The most successful negotiators are those who view their counterparts not as adversaries but as partners in a journey towards a common goal. They understand that a successful negotiation is one where both parties leave the table feeling understood, respected, and satisfied.

Sales negotiation is a multifaceted process combining psychology, strategy, and human connection. Each negotiation is a story, a unique blend of needs, desires, and personalities coming together to write a mutually beneficial conclusion. Welcome to the world of sales negotiation, where every conversation is an opportunity to connect, learn, and create enduring value.

The Role of Negotiation in the Sales Process

The role of sales negotiation is akin to the conductor of an orchestra, where every instrument has its unique sound, yet when played in harmony, creates a masterpiece. In the world of business, sales negotiation is that symphony – a blend of tactics, psychology, and human connection, all directed towards the crescendo of a successful deal.

Sales negotiation is not just a phase in the selling process; it's the heart of it. Imagine a bazaar in an ancient city where merchants and customers haggle over goods. Each exchange is a mini-drama, a play of words and emotions, where both parties aim for a satisfying finale. This timeless scenario exemplifies the essence of sales negotiation - a dynamic interaction aimed at achieving a win-win outcome.

Take the example of a small business owner negotiating with suppliers. The goal isn't just to lower costs but to build a relationship that ensures quality and reliability. In this dance, each step – from the initial offer to the final handshake – is a strategic move. It's like a chess game where each player anticipates the other's moves and adjusts their strategy accordingly.

Sales negotiation also plays a critical role in customer relationships. Imagine a salesperson negotiating with a potential client. This isn't merely a transaction; it's an opportunity to understand the client's needs, fears, and motivations. It's about finding common ground where the client's needs align with the product's benefits. The salesperson, in this scenario, is not just a negotiator but a consultant, guiding the client towards a decision that benefits both.

In the B2B (business-to-business) world, the role of sales negotiation takes on even greater significance. Consider a technology firm negotiating a service contract with a large corporation. The stakes are high, the negotiations complex, involving multiple layers of discussion around pricing, service levels, and contractual terms. Here, negotiation is a delicate balancing act – respecting the client's constraints while protecting one's own interests.

Furthermore, sales negotiation is a key driver of innovation. It pushes companies to tailor their offerings, innovate their products, and rethink their strategies. For instance, a company might negotiate with a client who needs a customized solution. This negotiation can lead the company to develop new features or services, thus enhancing its overall market offering.

Sales negotiation also has a profound impact on building long-term business relationships. A successful negotiation lays the foundation for trust, respect, and future business. It's not just about closing a deal; it's about opening doors to future opportunities.

In conclusion, the role of sales negotiation in the business world is multifaceted and vital. It's a dance of mutual benefit, a game of strategy, and a pathway to building lasting relationships. Each negotiation is a story of challenge, understanding, and compromise, culminating in a successful deal. This 500-word exploration into the role of sales negotiation shows that it's not just a skill but a crucial business tool, weaving the fabric of successful business relationships, one thread at a time.

The Common Misconception: "It's All About Price"

Let us understand the few misconceptions that prevail in the minds of negotiators:

1. Negotiation as a Battle: There's a common myth that negotiation is akin to a war where one must win at the other's expense. Imagine a medieval duel of wits! However, the truth is more like a collaborative dance. Successful negotiations focus on achieving a win-win outcome where both parties leave satisfied.
2. Negotiators are Born, Not Made: Just like the myth of the 'born artist', many believe that great negotiators are naturally gifted. The reality is that negotiation is a skill that can be developed and honed over time. Anyone can learn the nuances of negotiation through practice and perseverance.
3. Negotiation Equals Manipulation: Often, there's a perception that negotiation is all about trickery and manipulation, like a magician's sleight of hand. In fact, effective negotiation is built on trust, transparency, and genuinely understanding and addressing the needs of the other party.

4. Lowest Price Wins: It's a common belief that the main goal of negotiation is to get the lowest price. However, negotiation is more about value than just cost. Factors like quality, service, and long-term relationships often outweigh the benefit of a mere low price.
5. Negotiation as a One-Time Event: Many view negotiation as a single, isolated transaction. In contrast, negotiation is an ongoing process, part of building a lasting relationship. Like a series in a captivating book, each negotiation sets the stage for future interactions.
6. No Room for Emotions in Negotiation: It's a widespread belief that emotions should be left out of the negotiation process. Contrary to this, emotions play a crucial role. Good negotiators understand and harness emotions such as empathy, respect, and trust to foster a positive and productive negotiation environment.
7. More Information Means More Power: There's a notion that the party with the most information always has the upper hand. While being informed is crucial, negotiation is more about how you use that information to understand and align with the other party's needs and interests.
8. Aggressive Tactics Yield Results: Some believe that being aggressive or hard-nosed is the key to successful negotiation. However, aggression can backfire, damaging relationships and trust. Effective negotiation often involves a balance of assertiveness and cooperation.
9. The First Offer Always Loses: A common myth is that making the first offer puts you at a disadvantage as if you've shown your cards too soon. On the contrary, making the first

offer can set the anchor point around which the negotiation revolves, often giving you an advantage.
10. Negotiation Skills are only for Salespeople: It's easy to think that only those in sales need negotiation skills. In truth, negotiation is a part of everyday life – from discussing a raise with your boss to deciding on dinner plans with family. Everyone benefits from honing their negotiation skills.
11. Success in Negotiation is measured only in terms of the Deal: Many gauge the success of a negotiation solely by whether the deal was closed or not. Successful negotiation is also about the learning experience, relationship building, and setting the stage for future interactions.

Through our journey in the dynamic landscape of sales negotiation, we will uncover its pivotal role in the sales process and debunk several common misconceptions. Far from being a mere transactional step, sales negotiation emerges as a vital symphony of strategy, empathy, and human connection, essential to the rhythm of successful sales. This fascinating interplay, where misconceptions are dispelled, reveals negotiation as an art form, blending psychology, skill, and a dash of creativity. We will see how it's not a battleground but a collaborative event, where success is measured not just in closed deals but in lasting relationships and mutual satisfaction. As you eagerly turn the pages to the next chapters, you're poised to dive deeper into this intriguing world. We shall together explore the nuances, strategies, and real-life applications of sales negotiation, illuminating its role as a cornerstone in the edifice of business success. So, buckle up and prepare to be captivated by the unfolding saga of sales negotiation, a journey that promises to be as enlightening as it is exhilarating!

CHAPTER 2

PREPARING FOR SALES NEGOTIATION

*I*n sales negotiation, the journey to success begins long before the first conversation or meeting. It starts with meticulous preparation, the kind that transforms you from a mere seller into a trusted advisor and strategic negotiator. In this chapter, we'll dive into the crucial steps of preparing for sales negotiation, equipping you with the knowledge and strategies to set the stage for victory.

Researching Your Customer: The Foundation of Sales Success

In the intricate world of sales negotiation, success doesn't begin at the negotiation table; it starts much earlier with a crucial phase known as "researching your customer." This is the foundation upon which you build trust, tailor your approach and craft solutions that resonate with your prospect's deepest needs and aspirations. It's a journey of exploration, understanding, and insight that sets the stage for effective sales negotiations.

The Significance of Research

Researching your customer isn't merely a preliminary step; it's a strategic imperative. In a marketplace inundated with choices and information, the ability to differentiate yourself and your offering hinges on your knowledge of the prospect. Here's why it's of paramount importance:

1. Establishing Credibility: Informed conversations instill confidence in your prospect. It shows that you're not just a salesperson but a knowledgeable advisor.
2. Personalisation: Tailoring your approach based on customer research demonstrates that you view them as more than just another sale. It fosters a sense of importance and relevance.
3. Anticipating Needs: Research allows you to anticipate your customer's needs and concerns, addressing them proactively.
4. Competitive Advantage: In a competitive landscape, thorough research can provide you with insights that competitors may overlook.

The Art of Customer Research

Effective customer research goes beyond a cursory glance at a prospect's website or LinkedIn profile. It's a multidimensional exploration that uncovers insights about their business, industry, challenges, goals, and even their personal preferences and values. Here's how you can master the art of customer research:

1. Company Research:
   - Business Model: Understand the prospect's business model, including their products or services, target audience, and revenue streams.
   - Financial Health: Look for financial reports or news articles that shed light on the company's financial health and growth trajectory.
   - Competitive Landscape: Identify key competitors in their industry to gain insights into the competitive pressures they face.
   - Strategic Initiatives: Explore any recent strategic initiatives, acquisitions, or partnerships that might impact their needs.

2. Industry Analysis:
   - Trends: Stay updated on industry trends and shifts that could affect your prospect's business. This demonstrates your industry knowledge.
   - Challenges: Understand common challenges and pain points faced by businesses in their industry.
   - Regulatory Environment: Be aware of any relevant regulations or compliance issues that might impact your solution.

3. Prospect's Role and Responsibilities:
   - Decision-Maker Identification: Determine who the key decision-makers are within the prospect's organization. Are they the ultimate decision-makers, or do they report to someone else?
   - Goals and Objectives: Identify the prospect's personal and professional goals. What are they trying to achieve in their role?

- Challenges: Understand the challenges they face in their position, as addressing these can be a key selling point.
4. Previous Interactions:
   - Review Past Communications: If there have been previous interactions between your company and the prospect, review them to gain insights into their preferences and concerns.
   - Feedback: Check if there has been any feedback or comments from the prospect about your company or solutions.
5. Social Media and Online Presence:
   - LinkedIn: Explore their LinkedIn profile to learn about their professional background, connections, and any shared interests or affiliations.
   - Twitter and Blogs: Check if they are active on platforms like Twitter or have written blogs or articles that reveal their thoughts and perspectives.

Navigating the Research Landscape

Imagine you're selling cybersecurity solutions to a mid-sized healthcare provider. Effective research here would involve understanding not only the prospect's specific needs but also the broader healthcare landscape, regulatory requirements (such as HIPAA-Health Insurance Profitability and Accountability Act), and recent cyber threats targeting healthcare organizations.

You might uncover that the prospect recently suffered a data breach, leading to patient data exposure and regulatory fines. Armed with this information, you can tailor your approach to highlight how your cybersecurity solution addresses their immediate pain points and offers a robust defence against future breaches. You could also emphasize compliance features that align with healthcare regulations.

Why Mastery of Customer Research Matters

The mastery of customer research is the linchpin of successful sales negotiations. Here's why it matters:

1. Relevance: Thorough research ensures that your approach and messaging are highly relevant to the prospect's needs and challenges.
2. Trust Building: Informed conversations establish trust by demonstrating your credibility and understanding of their industry.
3. Anticipation: Research enables you to anticipate objections, concerns, and needs, allowing you to proactively address them.
4. Differentiation: It differentiates you from competitors who may not invest the same level of effort in understanding the prospect.
5. Personalization: Tailoring your approach based on research fosters a sense of personalization, making the prospect feel valued and understood.

In the exciting world of sales negotiation, "Researching Your Customer" is the opening chapter—a chapter where you embark on a journey of discovery and understanding. It's a journey that transforms you from a salesperson into a trusted advisor.

Setting Clear Objectives: The North Star of Sales Success

In the intricate world of sales negotiation, setting clear objectives serves as the North Star guiding your journey. It's the compass that ensures you stay on course, maintain focus, and achieve meaningful outcomes. The art of negotiation isn't just about engaging in conversations; it's about knowing precisely what you aim to achieve with each interaction. This is where "Setting Clear Objectives" comes into play—a foundational phase that lays the groundwork for successful negotiations.

The Importance of Clear Objectives

"Setting Clear Objectives" is not a mere formality; it's a strategic imperative. It's the foundation upon which every negotiation is built. Here's why it's of paramount importance:

1. Clarity of Purpose: Clear objectives provide you with a clear sense of purpose and direction. They define what you want to accomplish in the negotiation.
2. Focus and Efficiency: When you have well-defined objectives, you avoid meandering conversations and stay focused on what truly matters. This enhances the efficiency of your negotiations.
3. Alignment: Objectives align your efforts with the broader goals of your organization. They ensure that each negotiation contributes to your company's growth and success.
4. Measurement and Accountability: Clear objectives enable you to measure the success of your negotiations objectively. They also hold you accountable for achieving the desired outcomes.

The Art of Setting Objectives

Effective objective setting is a nuanced process that goes beyond merely stating what you want. It involves a deep understanding of your prospect, their needs, and the broader context of the negotiation. Here's how you can master the art of setting clear objectives:

1. Define Desired Outcomes: Start by defining the specific outcomes you want to achieve in the negotiation. These outcomes should be tangible and measurable.
2. Understand Prospect Needs: To set objectives effectively, you must understand your prospect's needs, challenges, and aspirations. What are they trying to accomplish, and how can your solution help them?
3. Prioritize Objectives: Not all objectives are created equal. Prioritize them based on their importance and relevance to both your organization and the prospect.
4. Consider Potential Trade-Offs: Recognize that some objectives may conflict with others. Consider potential trade-offs and be prepared to adjust your objectives as the negotiation progresses.
5. Define a BATNA: BATNA, or Best Alternative to a Negotiated Agreement, is the course of action you'll take if the negotiation doesn't lead to a satisfactory outcome. Having a well-defined BATNA can help you set realistic objectives.
6. Establish a Timeline: Determine the timeline for achieving your objectives. Are there specific deadlines or time-sensitive factors to consider?
7. Communicate Objectives Clearly: Ensure that your team and, if appropriate, the prospect are aware of your objectives. Clear communication fosters alignment.

Navigating the Objective-Setting Landscape

Imagine you're negotiating a contract with a software vendor for your company. To set clear objectives, you'd begin by defining your desired outcomes. These might include:

1. Cost Reduction: Negotiate a lower price or more favourable payment terms to reduce costs for your organization.
2. Service Level Agreement (SLA) Improvements: Aim to secure a higher level of service or support in the contract to ensure the software meets your company's needs.
3. Flexibility: Negotiate for flexibility in the contract terms to accommodate potential changes in your company's requirements.
4. Long-Term Relationship: Express your interest in building a long-term partnership with the vendor to foster cooperation and value creation beyond the current deal.

By setting these objectives, you have a clear roadmap for the negotiation. You know what you're aiming to achieve, which allows you to prepare accordingly and engage in productive discussions with the vendor.

Why Mastery of Objective Setting Matters

The mastery of objective setting is the keystone of successful sales negotiations. Here's why it matters:

1. Focus and Efficiency: Clear objectives keep you focused on what's essential, making your negotiations more efficient and effective.

2. Alignment: Objectives ensure that your negotiations align with your organization's strategic goals, contributing to overall success.
3. Measurement: Well-defined objectives provide a yardstick for measuring the success of your negotiations, allowing you to assess performance objectively.
4. Adaptability: While objectives provide direction, they also allow for adaptability. You can adjust your approach as the negotiation unfolds, provided it aligns with your objectives.
5. Confidence: Setting objectives instills confidence in your negotiation team. It clarifies what needs to be accomplished, reducing uncertainty.

"Setting Clear Objectives" is the prologue that defines the purpose and direction of your journey. It's the point where strategy meets action and where the negotiation roadmap takes shape. Mastery of this phase ensures that each negotiation is purposeful, efficient, and aligned with your organization's goals. It transforms the negotiation table from a place of uncertainty into a platform where success is not just hoped for but planned and pursued with clarity and determination.

Building Your Value Proposition: Crafting the Persuasive Heart of Sales

During the journey of sales negotiation, the value proposition stands as the beating heart of your offering—a compelling narrative that resonates with your prospect's needs, aspirations, and desires. It's the art of articulating the unique value your product or service brings to the table. This is where "Building

Your Value Proposition" comes into play—a pivotal phase that defines why your solution is not just desirable but indispensable.

The Essence of Value Proposition

Building your value proposition is not a mere exercise in marketing jargon; it's a strategic imperative. It's about crystallizing the benefits and advantages of your offering in a way that speaks directly to your prospect. Here's why it's of paramount importance:

1. Differentiation: A well-crafted value proposition sets you apart from competitors. It highlights what makes your solution unique and superior.
2. Relevance: It ensures that your offering is highly relevant to the prospect's needs and challenges. A strong value proposition answers the "What's in it for me?" question definitively.
3. Persuasion: Your value proposition is your persuasive tool. It convinces the prospect that your solution is the best fit for their specific requirements.
4. Clarity: A clear value proposition simplifies complex ideas and features, making it easier for the prospect to understand and appreciate the benefits.

The Art of Building a Value Proposition

Creating a compelling value proposition is an art that requires a deep understanding of your prospect, their pain points, and the unique strengths of your offering. Here's how you can master the art of building a persuasive value proposition:

1. Understand Your Prospect: Begin by understanding your prospect's needs, challenges, and goals. What keeps them up at night, and how can your solution address those concerns?
2. Identify Unique Benefits: Determine the unique benefits of your product or service. What sets it apart from competitors, and how does it solve the prospect's problems?
3. Quantify Value: Whenever possible, quantify the value your solution provides. This could be in terms of cost savings, efficiency gains, or revenue increases.
4. Speak the Prospect's Language: Craft your value proposition using language that resonates with your prospect. Avoid jargon and technical terms that may confuse or alienate them.
5. Address Pain Points: Highlight how your solution specifically addresses the prospect's pain points and challenges. Paint a vivid picture of how their life or business improves with your offering.
6. Keep It Concise: A value proposition should be concise and to the point. Avoid lengthy explanations and focus on the most impactful benefits.
7. Test and Refine: Continuously test and refine your value proposition based on feedback from prospects and the performance of your sales efforts.

Navigating the Value Proposition Landscape

Imagine you're selling project management software to a fast-growing start-up. Your research reveals that the prospect's pain points include project delays, communication gaps, and resource allocation challenges. To build a compelling value proposition, you could craft it as follows:

-Value Proposition:

Our project management software empowers your startup to conquer project delays, streamline team communication, and optimize resource allocation. With our intuitive platform, you'll experience:

- Faster Project Delivery: Eliminate bottlenecks and delays, ensuring projects are delivered on time and within budget.
- Effortless Collaboration: Enhance team communication and collaboration, fostering a more productive and innovative work environment.
- Resource Optimization: Maximize resource allocation, ensuring that your talented team is always focused on high-impact tasks.
- Scalability: Grow your start-up with confidence, knowing that our software scales seamlessly with your evolving needs.

This value proposition succinctly communicates how your solution addresses the start-up's specific pain points and offers tangible benefits.

Why Mastery of Value Proposition Matters

The mastery of building a value proposition is the cornerstone of successful sales negotiations. Here's why it matters:

1. Differentiation: A compelling value proposition sets you apart from competitors, making your offering more attractive.
2. Relevance: It ensures that your solution is highly relevant to the prospect's needs, increasing the likelihood of a successful sale.

3. Persuasion: Your value proposition is your persuasive tool. It convinces the prospect that your solution is the best choice for them.
4. Clarity: A clear value proposition simplifies complex ideas, making it easier for the prospect to understand and appreciate the benefits.

"Building Your Value Proposition" is the domain where your offering transforms from a collection of features into a persuasive force. It's where you distill the essence of why your solution matters, why it's worth investing in, and why it's the key to unlocking the prospect's desired outcomes. It's not just about presenting a product or service; it's about presenting value and making a compelling case for why your prospect should choose you over all other options. Mastery of this phase ensures that your offering is not just seen but celebrated as the answer to the prospect's needs and aspirations.

Identifying Potential Challenges: Navigating the Roadblocks to Sales Success

In the exciting world of sales negotiation, the ability to foresee and address potential challenges is akin to being an astute navigator, expertly charting a course through treacherous waters. Identifying these hurdles early in the process is not just a defensive strategy; it's a proactive approach to ensuring successful outcomes. This is where "Identifying Potential Challenges" becomes a crucial phase, allowing you to anticipate, prepare for, and ultimately overcome the obstacles that may arise.

The Significance of Identifying Challenges

Identifying potential challenges is more than a checklist of potential pitfalls; it's a strategic imperative. It's about recognizing that no negotiation is without its complexities and roadblocks. Here's why it's of paramount importance:

1. Proactive Preparation: Identifying challenges in advance allows you to proactively prepare for them. This reduces the likelihood of being caught off guard during the negotiation.
2. Mitigation Strategies: Knowing the potential challenges enables you to develop mitigation strategies. You can create contingency plans or alternative approaches to address these issues effectively.
3. Enhanced Communication: Being aware of potential challenges fosters open and transparent communication with the prospect. It demonstrates your commitment to resolving issues and finding mutually beneficial solutions.
4. Relationship Building: Successfully addressing challenges can actually strengthen the relationship between you and the prospect. It showcases your dedication and problem-solving skills.

The Art of Identifying Potential Challenges

Effective challenge identification is not about pessimism but about realism. It involves a systematic assessment of various factors, including the prospect, your offering, and the broader context of the negotiation. Here's how you can master the art of identifying potential challenges:

1. Know Your Prospect: Understand your prospect's organization, industry, and specific challenges they face. What obstacles might they encounter in adopting your solution?
2. Review Historical Data: Examine data from previous negotiations or similar deals. Are there common challenges that tend to arise? What lessons can be learned from past experiences?
3. Consult with Your Team: Involve your sales team, product experts, and other stakeholders in identifying potential challenges. They may offer valuable insights based on their expertise.
4. Evaluate Market Conditions: Consider the current market conditions, economic factors, and industry trends. How might external factors impact the negotiation?
5. Anticipate Objections: Think about objections the prospect might raise during the negotiation. These objections often reveal potential challenges that need to be addressed.
6. Analyse the Competition: Study your competitors and their offerings. What challenges might arise if the prospect is considering multiple options?
7. Legal and Compliance Issues: Be aware of legal and compliance requirements that may affect the negotiation. Failure to address these can lead to significant challenges.
8. Cultural and Communication Factors: Consider cultural differences or communication challenges that may arise if you're dealing with international clients.

Navigating the Challenge Identification Landscape

Imagine you're selling a software solution to a large financial institution. Your research reveals that potential challenges might include:

1. Security Concerns: The institution has strict cybersecurity requirements, and any software solution must meet stringent security standards. Failure to address these concerns could be a major roadblock.
2. Integration Complexity: The institution's existing IT infrastructure is complex, with multiple legacy systems. Ensuring seamless integration with your software might be a challenge.
3. Budget Constraints: The institution is operating under budget constraints, and they may have reservations about the cost of your solution.
4. Compliance and Regulatory Hurdles: The financial industry is heavily regulated, and the institution must ensure that any software solution complies with regulatory requirements.

By identifying these potential challenges, you can proactively prepare for the negotiation. You might engage your technical team to address security concerns, develop a clear integration plan, and explore flexible pricing options to accommodate budget constraints.

Why Mastery in Challenge Identification Matters

The mastery of challenge identification is the keystone of successful sales negotiations. Here's why it matters:

1. Proactive Preparation: Identifying challenges in advance allows you to proactively prepare for them, reducing the risk of being blindsided during negotiations.
2. Mitigation Strategies: Armed with knowledge, you can develop mitigation strategies to address challenges effectively, increasing the likelihood of a successful outcome.
3. Enhanced Communication: Being aware of potential challenges fosters open and transparent communication with the prospect, demonstrating your commitment to problem-solving.
4. Relationship Building: Successfully addressing challenges can strengthen the relationship between you and the prospect, showcasing your dedication and expertise.

Identifying potential challenges is the path where you put on your strategist's hat and chart a course that anticipates the twists and turns of the negotiation journey. It's where you demonstrate your commitment to problem-solving and your ability to navigate even the most complex terrain. It's not about avoiding challenges but about embracing them as opportunities to showcase your expertise, dedication, and ability to find mutually beneficial solutions. Mastery of this phase ensures that the negotiation table is a place where roadblocks become stepping stones and where success is not just a hope but a well-prepared plan.

CHAPTER 3

BUILDING RAPPORT AND TRUST

*I*n the vibrant landscape of sales negotiation, the foundation of success rests upon the pillars of rapport and trust. This pivotal phase is where the seeds of credibility, understanding, and mutual respect are sown. It's the art of fostering genuine connections and building unwavering trust with your prospects. As we delve into building rapport and trust, we explore the strategies and nuances that transform mere business interactions into enduring partnerships. From active listening to empathy and transparent communication, this chapter is your guide to establishing the crucial bonds that underpin successful sales negotiations.

The Importance of Trust in Sales: The Cornerstone of Success

In the complex and dynamic world of sales, trust emerges as the bedrock upon which all successful relationships and transactions are built. Whether you're closing a deal with a new prospect or nurturing a long-term client relationship, trust is the currency that facilitates productive interactions and fosters loyalty. This chapter explores the importance of trust in sales, shedding light on why trust is not merely desirable but an absolute necessity for sales professionals.

Trust as the Foundation

Trust is not a peripheral aspect of sales; it's the very foundation upon which all meaningful interactions rest. Here's why trust occupies such a paramount role:

1. Credibility and Authority: Trust establishes you as a credible and authoritative figure in the eyes of your prospects. It's the difference between being seen as a salesperson and being perceived as a trusted advisor.
2. Open Communication: Trust creates an environment where open and honest communication can flourish. Prospects are more likely to share their needs, concerns, and objectives when they trust you.
3. Risk Mitigation: Trust reduces perceived risk for prospects. They feel more secure in their decision-making when they have confidence in your expertise and integrity.
4. Relationship Building: Trust is the linchpin of relationship building. It transforms a transactional encounter into a lasting partnership. Long-term clients often stem from trust forged during the initial sale.
5. Competitive Edge: In a competitive marketplace, trust can be the decisive factor that sets you apart. When prospects trust you, they're more likely to choose your offering over alternatives.

The Building Blocks of Trust

Trust is not a monolithic concept but a collection of attributes and behaviours. Building trust involves the consistent demonstration of these essential building blocks:

1. Reliability: Reliability is the cornerstone of trust. It means delivering on your promises consistently. This includes meeting deadlines, honouring agreements, and providing a dependable product or service.
2. Integrity: Integrity entails being honest and ethical in all your dealings. Trust erodes quickly when prospects detect dishonesty or unethical behaviour.
3. Competence: Competence involves demonstrating expertise in your field. It reassures prospects that you have the knowledge and skills needed to fulfill their needs.
4. Transparency: Transparency means being open and forthright in your communication. It includes disclosing relevant information, even if it may not be in your immediate favour.
5. Empathy: Empathy is the ability to understand and relate to your prospect's emotions and perspective. It shows that you genuinely care about their concerns.
6. Consistency: Consistency involves maintaining a uniform and dependable approach in your interactions. It reinforces the perception of reliability and dependability.
7. Communication: Effective communication is key to building trust. It involves active listening, clear articulation of your offerings, and addressing prospect concerns promptly and comprehensively.

Trust in the Sales Cycle

Trust is not a one-time achievement; it's a continuous process that evolves throughout the sales cycle:

1. Trust Building in Prospecting: During the prospecting phase, your initial interactions set the tone for trust. Demonstrating respect for the prospect's time and needs builds credibility from the outset.
2. Trust in Needs Analysis: In the discovery phase, thorough needs analysis showcases your commitment to understanding the prospect's specific challenges. This builds trust by demonstrating empathy and competence.
3. Trust in Presentation: A well-prepared and tailored presentation highlights your competence and the value your solution offers. It instills confidence in your prospects.
4. Trust in Handling Objections: Effective objection handling demonstrates your integrity and commitment to addressing concerns. It reassures the prospect that you're acting in their best interest.
5. Trust in Closing: In the closing phase, prospects need to trust that their decision to move forward is the right one. Your professionalism and transparency are vital in cementing that trust.
6. Trust in Post-Sale Support: Even after the sale, trust remains critical. Delivering on promises, providing exceptional support, and consistently exceeding expectations fortify the client's trust and can lead to repeat business and referrals.

Trust and Long-Term Success

In the grand narrative of sales, trust is the thread that weaves together the various chapters of your career. Long-term success in sales is intricately tied to the trust you cultivate with clients and prospects over time. Here's why trust is the key to enduring success:

1. Repeat Business: Clients who trust you are more likely to return for additional purchases. They know that you'll deliver on your promises and provide value.
2. Referrals: Trust leads to referrals. Satisfied clients who trust your recommendations are more inclined to refer their contacts to you.
3. Resilience in Challenges: When challenges arise—such as economic downturns or market fluctuations—clients are more likely to remain loyal to a trusted advisor.
4. Leveraging Trust for Growth: Trust can be leveraged to expand your client base and explore new opportunities within existing accounts. It's the bridge to upselling and cross-selling.
5. Professional Fulfillment: Building trust and nurturing long-term relationships can be professionally fulfilling. Knowing that you've made a positive impact on clients' lives and businesses is rewarding.

The significance of Trust is the underlying theme that defines your journey. It's not just about closing deals but about fostering enduring partnerships. It's about becoming more than a salesperson; it's about becoming a trusted advisor. It's a testament to your integrity, competence, and commitment to your clients' successes. In a world where choices abound, trust is the beacon that guides prospects and clients to you, time and time again. It's not just the cornerstone of success; it's the path to sustained excellence in the world of sales.

Establishing Credibility: The Art of Trust and Expertise

In the dynamic realm of sales negotiation, credibility is the currency that can open doors, instill confidence, and lay the foundation for successful interactions. This chapter explores the art of establishing credibility, shedding light on why credibility is not just a desirable attribute but an essential component of a sales professional's toolkit.

The Significance of Credibility

"Establishing Credibility" is not a superficial act but a strategic imperative. It's about demonstrating that you are a trustworthy and knowledgeable resource whom prospects can rely on. Here's why credibility holds such a paramount role:

1. Trust Building: Credibility is the cornerstone of trust. When prospects believe in your credibility, they are more likely to trust your recommendations and engage in open, honest conversations.
2. Authority: Credibility positions you as an authority in your field. It conveys to prospects that you possess the expertise needed to guide them effectively.
3. Competitive Advantage: In a competitive marketplace, credibility can set you apart from others offering similar products or services. It becomes a key differentiator.

4. Risk Mitigation: Credibility reduces the perceived risk for prospects. When they trust your expertise and integrity, they are more comfortable making decisions that involve an investment, whether of time, money, or resources.
5. Relationship Building: Credibility is a linchpin of relationship building. It paves the way for long-term partnerships, where clients return to you as a trusted advisor.

The Building Blocks of Credibility

Credibility is not an innate trait; it's a collection of attributes and behaviours that you can cultivate and showcase. Building credibility involves consistent demonstration of these essential building blocks:

1. Expertise: Expertise is the foundation of credibility. It involves in-depth knowledge of your field, industry, and product or service. Being well-informed and staying current in your domain establishes you as a credible source.
2. Honesty and Integrity: Honesty and integrity are non-negotiable. Uphold ethical standards in all your dealings, and always be truthful and transparent. A single breach of trust can tarnish your credibility irreparably.
3. Consistency: Consistency in your actions and messaging reinforces your credibility. Prospects and clients need to see a pattern of reliability and dependability over time.
4. Communication: Effective communication is key to establishing credibility. Clearly articulate your expertise, ideas, and solutions. Listen actively to understand your prospect's needs and concerns.

5. Empathy: Empathy is the ability to understand and relate to your prospect's emotions and perspective. It shows that you genuinely care about their concerns and objectives.
6. Problem-Solving: Demonstrate your problem-solving skills by providing innovative solutions to your prospect's challenges. Show that you're not just selling a product but helping them achieve their goals.
7. Client Success Stories: Share success stories and case studies that highlight how your expertise has benefited other clients. Real-world examples validate your credibility.

Credibility Across the Sales Cycle

Establishing credibility is an ongoing process that evolves throughout the sales cycle:

1. Credibility in Prospecting: During prospecting, your initial interactions set the tone for credibility. Respect your prospect's time and needs. Be well-prepared and knowledgeable about your offering.
2. Credibility in Needs Analysis: In the discovery phase, credibility is built by conducting a thorough needs analysis. Show that you understand the prospect's specific challenges and objectives.
3. Credibility in Presentation: In the presentation phase, your credibility is on display as you demonstrate how your solution addresses the prospect's needs. Knowledge, clarity, and empathy are paramount.
4. Credibility in Handling Objections: Effective objection handling showcases your credibility. Address concerns with professionalism and honesty, offering viable solutions.

5. Credibility in Closing: In the closing phase, your credibility is essential in assuring the prospect that their decision to move forward is the right one. Be transparent and reliable in finalizing the deal.
6. Credibility in Post-Sale Support: Even after the sale, credibility remains critical. Deliver on promises, provide exceptional support, and consistently exceed expectations to strengthen your credibility.

Leveraging Credibility for Success

Credibility is not just a static attribute; it's a dynamic asset that can be leveraged to achieve greater success:

1. Repeat Business: Clients who trust your credibility are more likely to return for additional purchases. They know that you'll deliver on your promises and provide value.
2. Referrals: Credibility leads to referrals. Satisfied clients who trust your expertise are more inclined to refer their contacts to you.
3. Resilience in Challenges: When challenges arise—such as economic downturns or market fluctuations—clients are more likely to remain loyal to a credible advisor.
4. Professional Fulfillment: Building credibility and nurturing long-term relationships can be professionally fulfilling. Knowing that you've made a positive impact on clients' lives and businesses is rewarding.
5. Market Influence: Credibility can extend beyond individual interactions to influence market perceptions. As a credible figure in your field, your recommendations and insights can carry weight in the industry.

Establishing credibility is that specialised domain where your expertise is not just acknowledged but celebrated. It's not about showcasing your knowledge for its own sake but about using it to guide and benefit your prospects. It's where you transform from a salesperson into a trusted advisor—a role that transcends transactions and encompasses partnerships. In a world where information is abundant but trust is scarce, credibility becomes your most valuable asset. It's not just the path to success; it's the path to becoming a beacon of trust and expertise in the realm of sales.

Effective Communication Techniques: The Art of Persuasion and Connection

In the vibrant world of sales negotiation, effective communication stands as the linchpin that connects sales professionals with their prospects and clients. This chapter delves into the art of effective communication techniques, emphasizing the pivotal role they play in building rapport, conveying value, and ultimately securing successful outcomes in sales.

The Significance of Effective Communication

"Effective Communication Techniques" are not just a set of soft skills; they are the lifeblood of successful sales negotiations. Here's why effective communication holds such paramount importance:

1. Building Rapport: Effective communication is the key to building rapport with prospects. It fosters a sense of trust, understanding, and connection.

2. Conveying Value: Your ability to articulate the value of your product or service hinges on effective communication. You must convey how your offering meets the prospect's needs and solves their challenges.
3. Overcoming Objections: Effective communication helps you address objections and concerns confidently and persuasively. It allows you to navigate objections without derailing the negotiation.
4. Relationship Building: Strong client relationships are founded on effective communication. Clients need to feel heard, valued, and understood throughout the engagement.
5. Closing Deals: Ultimately, effective communication techniques are what enable you to close deals successfully. The art of persuasion, active listening, and clarity are critical in reaching mutually beneficial agreements.

The Building Blocks of Effective Communication

Effective communication is not a one-size-fits-all concept; it's a collection of strategies and skills that can be cultivated and refined. Building effective communication involves consistent demonstration of these essential building blocks:

1. Active Listening: Active listening involves giving your full attention to the speaker, seeking to understand their perspective, and refraining from interrupting. It shows respect and fosters rapport.
2. Clarity: Clear and concise communication is essential. Avoid jargon and ambiguity. Your messages should be easily understood by your audience.

3. Empathy: Empathy is the ability to understand and share the feelings of your prospect or client. It demonstrates that you care about their concerns and are committed to helping them.
4. Nonverbal Communication: Nonverbal cues, such as body language, facial expressions, and tone of voice, can convey important messages. Be mindful of your nonverbal communication to ensure it aligns with your verbal messages.
5. Adaptability: Effective communicators are adaptable. They tailor their communication style to suit the preferences and needs of their audience.
6. Persuasion: Persuasive communication involves presenting your ideas and recommendations in a compelling manner. It's about influencing your audience's beliefs or behaviours.
7. Timely and Relevant Information: Provide information that is timely and directly relevant to the prospect's needs and concerns. Avoid overwhelming them with irrelevant details.

Effective Communication Across the Sales Cycle

Effective communication is not a one-time effort but a continuous process that evolves throughout the sales cycle:

1. Effective Communication in Prospecting: In the prospecting phase, effective communication involves clearly articulating your value proposition and respecting the prospect's time and preferences.
2. Effective Communication in Needs Analysis: During the discovery phase, effective communication is about active listening and asking probing questions to understand the prospect's challenges and objectives fully.

3. Effective Communication in Presentation: In the presentation phase, effective communication includes presenting your solution clearly and persuasively, highlighting its benefits and value.
4. Effective Communication in Handling Objections: When objections arise, effective communication is essential to address them with empathy and persuasive responses.
5. Effective Communication in Closing: In the closing phase, your ability to communicate the terms of the deal, address any final concerns, and guide the prospect through the decision-making process is crucial.
6. Effective Communication in Post-Sale Support: Even after the sale, effective communication remains essential. You must continue to provide clear and helpful communication regarding implementation, support, and ongoing needs.

Leveraging Effective Communication for Success

Effective communication is not just a skill; it's a strategic advantage that can be leveraged for greater success:

1. Building Rapport: Effective communication techniques are the building blocks of rapport. By demonstrating active listening, empathy, and clear articulation, you can foster trust and connection.
2. Conveying Value: Your ability to convey the value of your product or service hinges on effective communication. A compelling message that aligns with the prospect's needs can be the tipping point in your favour.
3. Overcoming Objections: Effective communication is the key to addressing objections persuasively. It allows you to navigate

objections without creating friction and maintain the flow of the negotiation.
4. Relationship Building: Long-term client relationships are founded on effective communication. Clients need to feel heard, valued, and understood throughout the engagement.
5. Closing Deals: Ultimately, effective communication techniques are what enable you to close deals successfully. The art of persuasion, active listening, and clarity are critical in reaching mutually beneficial agreements.

Effective communication is a very specialised area where your words become more than just information; they become instruments of connection, understanding, and persuasion. It's not just about talking; it's about conveying value, addressing concerns, and building rapport. It's the gateway to transforming prospects into clients and clients into loyal advocates. In a world where information is abundant, it's your ability to communicate effectively that sets you apart as a skilled and trusted sales professional. It's not just a skill; it's your pathway to success in the realm of sales negotiation.

Building Long-Term Relationships: The Heartbeat of Sales Success

In the ever-evolving landscape of sales negotiation, the value of long-term relationships cannot be overstated. This chapter delves into the significance of long-term relationships, highlighting why they are not just desirable but the very essence of sustained success in sales.

The Significance of Long-Term Relationships

"Long-Term Relationships" are more than a buzzword; they are the lifeblood of a thriving sales career. Here's why they hold such paramount importance:

1. Trust and Loyalty: Long-term relationships are built on a foundation of trust and mutual understanding. Clients who trust you are more likely to remain loyal, returning for repeat business and referring others to your services.
2. Repeat Business: Long-term clients often translate into repeat business. They recognize the value you bring, and their ongoing needs create a steady stream of opportunities.
3. Referrals and Recommendations: Satisfied, long-term clients become your advocates. They are more inclined to refer their colleagues, friends, and associates to your services, extending your network and client base.
4. Resilience in Challenges: Long-term relationships weather challenges more effectively. When economic downturns or market fluctuations occur, clients with whom you share a history of success are more likely to stay the course with you.
5. Efficient Sales Process: With long-term clients, the sales process becomes more efficient. You have a deep understanding of their needs and preferences, enabling you to tailor solutions more effectively.

Nurturing Long-Term Relationships

Long-term relationships are not established overnight; they require consistent effort and dedication. Here's how to nurture and maintain them:

1. Open and Transparent Communication: Maintain open, transparent, and frequent communication with your clients. Keep them informed about new offerings, changes, and industry insights.
2. Exceed Expectations: Strive to exceed your clients' expectations consistently. Surprise them with exceptional service and value-added solutions.
3. Personalization: Tailor your interactions to your clients' unique preferences and needs. Show that you understand their specific challenges and goals.
4. Problem-Solving: Be proactive in identifying and addressing potential challenges or issues. Your ability to solve problems quickly and effectively builds trust.
5. Anticipate Needs: Stay ahead of your clients' needs by anticipating them. Proactively offer solutions that align with their evolving objectives.
6. Reliability: Be a reliable partner. Meet deadlines, honor agreements, and consistently deliver on your promises.

Long-Term Relationships Across the Sales Cycle

Long-term relationships are not limited to the post-sale phase; they are woven into every stage of the sales cycle:

1. Building Long-Term Relationships in Prospecting: Begin nurturing long-term relationships during prospecting by demonstrating respect, understanding, and a commitment to their success.
2. Building Long-Term Relationships in Needs Analysis: During the discovery phase, delve deep to understand your client's

challenges and objectives fully. Show that you're invested in their long-term success.
3. Building Long-Term Relationships in Presentation: In the presentation phase, focus on how your solution can deliver ongoing value. Articulate not just the immediate benefits but the long-term impact.
4. Building Long-Term Relationships in Handling Objections: Effective objection handling can strengthen long-term relationships. Address concerns with professionalism and honesty.
5. Building Long-Term Relationships in Closing: During the closing phase, communicate the long-term benefits of the deal. Reiterate your commitment to their success beyond the immediate transaction.
6. Building Long-Term Relationships in Post-Sale Support: Post-sale support is a crucial aspect of nurturing long-term relationships. Provide exceptional service, proactive communication, and continuous value.

Leveraging Long-Term Relationships for Success

Long-term relationships are not just a pleasant by-product of sales; they are a strategic asset that can be leveraged for greater success:

1. Repeat Business: Long-term clients are more likely to return for additional purchases. Their trust in your services and ongoing needs create opportunities for repeat business.
2. Referrals and Recommendations: Satisfied, long-term clients are your advocates. They are more inclined to refer others to your services, expanding your network and client base.

3. Resilience in Challenges: Long-term relationships provide stability and resilience during challenging times. Clients who trust you are more likely to stay loyal, even when faced with economic or market uncertainties.
4. Efficient Sales Process: With long-term clients, the sales process becomes more efficient. You have a deep understanding of their needs and preferences, enabling you to tailor solutions more effectively.
5. Professional Fulfillmet: Nurturing long-term relationships can be professionally fulfilling. Knowing that you've made a positive, ongoing impact on clients' lives and businesses is rewarding.

"Long-Term Relationships" is the platform where transactions evolve into meaningful partnerships. It's where your role transcends that of a salesperson to that of a trusted advisor and partner. It's about cultivating bonds that stand the test of time and flourish in the face of challenges. In a world where fleeting interactions abound, long-term relationships are a testament to your dedication, professionalism, and commitment to your clients' ongoing success. They are not just the outcome; they are the heartbeat of your sustained excellence in the realm of sales negotiation.

CHAPTER 4

INTRODUCTION TO THE ART OF LISTENING

*I*n the intricate realm of sales negotiation, the ability to listen transcends mere passive reception—it becomes a skill, an art, and a strategic advantage. "The Art of Listening" is a pivotal chapter that underscores the profound significance of active and empathetic listening in forging meaningful connections, uncovering hidden needs, and navigating the intricate dance of negotiations. Within these pages, we explore the transformative power of listening as a catalyst for building trust and understanding and, ultimately, achieving successful outcomes in the complex tapestry of sales.

Active Listening Skills: The Catalyst for Connection and Understanding

In the dynamic arena of sales negotiation, active listening skills stand as the cornerstone that can bridge the gap between sales professionals and their prospects or clients. This chapter explores the profound significance of active listening skills, emphasizing their pivotal role in building rapport, uncovering hidden needs, and orchestrating successful negotiations.

The Significance of Active Listening Skills

"Active Listening Skills" are not a mere courtesy; they are the bedrock upon which meaningful and productive interactions are built. Here's why active listening holds such paramount importance:

1. Building Rapport: Active listening is the key to building rapport with prospects or clients. It fosters trust, respect, and a sense of connection, setting a positive tone for negotiations.
2. Uncovering Hidden Needs: Active listening allows you to go beyond surface-level information. By tuning in to subtle cues and nuances in the conversation, you can uncover hidden needs, concerns, and priorities.
3. Problem Solving: Effective active listening facilitates problem-solving. By truly understanding your prospect's challenges, you can tailor your solutions to address their specific needs.
4. Conflict Resolution: In the event of conflicts or disputes during negotiations, active listening enables you to understand the root causes and work collaboratively toward resolutions.
5. Effective Communication: Active listening is a linchpin of effective communication. When you listen attentively, your responses become more relevant, thoughtful, and persuasive.

The Building Blocks of Active Listening Skills

Active listening skills are not innate; they are honed through practice and dedication. Building active listening skills involves consistent demonstration of these essential building blocks:

1. Attentive Presence: Be fully present in the conversation. Minimize distractions and focus on the speaker. Show that their words matter to you.
2. Empathetic Understanding: Try to see the world from the speaker's perspective. Understand their emotions, concerns, and objectives. Empathy fosters a deeper connection.
3. Nonverbal Cues: Pay attention to nonverbal cues, such as body language, facial expressions, and tone of voice. These can provide valuable insights into the speaker's feelings and intentions.
4. Clarification: Ask clarifying questions to ensure you have correctly understood the speaker's message. Avoid making assumptions or jumping to conclusions.
5. Reflective Responses: Reflect on what the speaker has said to confirm your understanding and show that you are actively engaged in the conversation.
6. Patience: Allow the speaker to express themselves fully without interruption. Avoid the urge to interject with your own thoughts or solutions prematurely.
7. Paraphrasing: Paraphrasing involves restating the speaker's message in your own words. It demonstrates that you are actively processing the information and seeking clarity.

Active Listening Skills Across the Sales Cycle

Active listening skills are not confined to a specific phase of the sales cycle; they are integral throughout the entire process:

1. Active Listening in Prospecting: In the prospecting phase, active listening involves understanding the prospect's needs, challenges, and objectives. This sets the stage for a meaningful and personalized approach.
2. Active Listening in Needs Analysis: During the discovery phase, active listening is essential. Ask probing questions and dig deep to uncover the prospect's underlying concerns and goals.
3. Active Listening in Presentation: In the presentation phase, active listening allows you to tailor your presentation to address the specific needs and priorities you've identified.
4. Active Listening in Handling Objections: Effective objection handling hinges on active listening. By understanding the nature of the objection and the underlying concerns, you can respond persuasively.
5. Active Listening in Closing: In the closing phase, active listening helps you address any lingering doubts or objections, allowing you to guide the prospect toward a confident decision.
6. Active Listening in Post-Sale Support: Even after the sale, active listening remains essential. Continue to listen to the client's feedback, concerns, and evolving needs to provide exceptional support and maintain a strong relationship.

Leveraging Active Listening Skills for Success

Active listening skills are not just a tool; they are a strategic advantage that can be leveraged for greater success:

1. Building Rapport: Active listening is the foundation of rapport. It fosters trust, respect, and a sense of connection that forms the basis for fruitful negotiations.
2. Uncovering Hidden Needs: Active listening goes beyond surface-level information. By tuning in to subtle cues and nuances in the conversation, you can uncover hidden needs, concerns, and priorities.
3. Problem Solving: Effective active listening facilitates problem-solving. By truly understanding your prospect's challenges, you can tailor your solutions to address their specific needs.
4. Conflict Resolution: In the event of conflicts or disputes during negotiations, active listening enables you to understand the root causes and work collaboratively toward resolutions.
5. Effective Communication: Active listening is a linchpin of effective communication. When you listen attentively, your responses become more relevant, thoughtful, and persuasive.

In the grand narrative of sales, "Active Listening Skills" is the segment where the role of a passive listener evolves into an active catalyst for connection and understanding. It's where you move beyond hearing words to comprehending the deeper meanings and motivations behind them. It's not just about listening; it's about showing that you care, that you're invested, and that you're genuinely committed to the prospect's or client's success. In a world where noise abounds, active listening skills are the instrument that harmonizes the conversations and orchestrates successful negotiations. They are not just skills; they are the catalysts that transform interactions into fruitful partnerships in the realm of sales negotiation.

Asking Powerful Questions: The Key to Insight and Influence

In the intricate domain of sales negotiation, the art of asking powerful questions emerges as a potent tool that enables sales professionals to gain deep insight, uncover latent needs, and guide prospects or clients toward mutually beneficial agreements. This chapter explores the profound significance of asking powerful questions, highlighting its pivotal role in building understanding, fostering engagement, and, ultimately, achieving successful outcomes in sales.

The Significance of Asking Powerful Questions

"Asking Powerful Questions" is not a mere conversational tactic; it is the compass that navigates sales professionals through the complex terrain of negotiations. Here's why asking powerful questions holds such paramount importance:

1. Gaining Insight: Powerful questions serve as gateways to understanding. They allow you to explore the prospect's or client's needs, objectives, and pain points in depth, providing valuable insight.
2. Uncovering Latent Needs: Beyond surface-level information, powerful questions help uncover latent needs—those challenges and aspirations that may not be immediately apparent but hold significant sway over decision-making.
3. Guiding the Conversation: By asking purposeful questions, you can guide the direction of the conversation, ensuring it remains focused on relevant topics and objectives.

4. Building Engagement: Engaging questions stimulate curiosity and encourage active participation from the prospect or client, fostering a sense of collaboration and shared problem-solving.
5. Demonstrating Expertise: Thoughtful questions demonstrate your expertise and industry knowledge, positioning you as a credible and valuable resource.

The Building Blocks of Asking Powerful Questions

Asking powerful questions is not a matter of coincidence; it's a skill that can be honed through practice and refinement. Building the ability to ask powerful questions involves consistent demonstration of these essential building blocks:

1. Curiosity: Cultivate a genuine curiosity about your prospect's or client's needs and goals. Approach each conversation with a mindset of exploration and discovery.
2. Active Listening: Active listening is the bedrock of powerful questioning. Pay close attention to the responses to your questions, using them to formulate follow-up inquiries.
3. Empathy: Put yourself in the shoes of your prospect or client. Understand their perspective and emotions, and frame questions that resonate with their experience.
4. Openness: Be open to unexpected answers and perspectives. Avoid leading questions that steer the conversation in a particular direction.
5. Clarity: Ensure your questions are clear and concise. Ambiguity can lead to confusion and hinder the effectiveness of the conversation.

6. Context Awareness: Consider the context and timing of your questions. Tailor them to the specific stage of the sales cycle and the prospect's or client's situation.
7. Respectful Inquiry: Show respect for the prospect's or client's time and preferences. Avoid bombarding them with a barrage of questions; instead, ask purposeful and relevant ones.

Asking Powerful Questions Across the Sales Cycle

Asking powerful questions is not limited to one phase of the sales cycle; it is a versatile tool that can be employed throughout the entire process:

1. During Prospecting: In the prospecting phase, powerful questions can help you understand the prospect's pain points and whether your offering aligns with their needs.
2. During Needs Analysis: During the discovery phase, powerful questions uncover the prospect's underlying challenges, objectives, and motivations, providing a comprehensive understanding.
3. During Presentation: In the presentation phase, powerful questions allow you to tailor your pitch to address the specific needs and priorities you've identified.
4. During Handling Objections: When objections arise, powerful questions help you delve deeper into the nature of the objection and the prospect's concerns, enabling more effective responses.
5. During Closing: In the closing phase, powerful questions can clarify any lingering doubts or objections and guide the prospect toward a confident decision.

6. During Post-Sale Support: Even after the sale, asking powerful questions remains invaluable. They help you understand the client's evolving needs and gather feedback for continuous improvement.

Leveraging Powerful Questions for Success

Asking powerful questions is not just a technique; it is a strategic advantage that can be leveraged for greater success:

1. Gaining Insight: Powerful questions enable you to gain deep insight into the prospect's or client's needs, motivations, and concerns. This insight guides your approach and recommendations.
2. Uncovering Latent Needs: Beyond surface-level information, powerful questions unearth latent needs—those challenges and aspirations that may not be immediately apparent but significantly influence decisions.
3. Guiding the Conversation: By asking purposeful questions, you can steer the direction of the conversation, ensuring it remains focused on relevant topics and objectives.
4. Building Engagement: Engaging questions stimulate curiosity and active participation, fostering a sense of collaboration and shared problem-solving.
5. Demonstrating Expertise: Thoughtful questions demonstrate your expertise and industry knowledge, positioning you as a credible and valuable resource.

In the grand narrative of sales, "Asking Powerful Questions" is the area where the role of an inquirer evolves into that of an insightful guide. It's where your questions become more than just words; they become instruments of discovery, connection, and persuasion. It's not just about asking; it's about asking with purpose, empathy, and clarity. In a world where information is abundant but insight is scarce, asking powerful questions is the compass that leads you toward deeper understanding and successful outcomes in the realm of sales negotiation. It's not just a skill; it's the key to insight and influence.

Uncovering Customer Needs and Pain Points: The Foundation of Effective Sales

In the intricate landscape of sales negotiation, the ability to uncover customer needs and pain points stands as the linchpin that separates average sales professionals from exceptional ones. This chapter delves into the profound significance of uncovering customer needs and pain points, emphasizing its pivotal role in building rapport, tailoring solutions, and, ultimately, achieving successful outcomes in sales.

The Significance of Uncovering Customer Needs and Pain Points

"Uncovering Customer Needs and Pain Points" is not a perfunctory step in the sales process; it is the catalyst that propels meaningful interactions and drives successful negotiations. Here's why it holds such paramount importance:

1. Building Rapport: Understanding a customer's needs and pain points fosters rapport. It shows that you are genuinely interested in their well-being and committed to addressing their concerns.

2. Tailoring Solutions: Armed with insights into a customer's needs and pain points, you can tailor your solutions to align perfectly with their objectives. This customization enhances the perceived value of your offerings.
3. Overcoming Objections: Knowing a customer's pain points equips you to anticipate objections and address them proactively. It demonstrates your expertise and problem-solving abilities.
4. Establishing Trust: Customers are more likely to trust a sales professional who takes the time to understand their unique challenges. Trust is the bedrock of successful negotiations.
5. Effective Communication: Uncovering needs and pain points leads to more effective communication. Your messages become relevant, resonant, and solution-oriented.

The Building Blocks of Uncovering Customer Needs and Pain Points

Uncovering customer needs and pain points is not a random endeavour; it's a skill that can be honed through a systematic approach. Building this ability involves consistent demonstration of these essential building blocks:

1. Active Listening: Active listening is the foundation of uncovering customer needs and pain points. Pay close attention to what the customer says, both in words and nonverbal cues.
2. Empathy: Put yourself in the customer's shoes. Understand their emotions, concerns, and objectives. Empathy fosters a deeper connection.

3. Probing Questions: Ask probing questions that go beyond surface-level information. Encourage the customer to share their challenges, aspirations, and priorities.
4. Observation: Observe the customer's behaviour and nonverbal cues. These can provide valuable insights into their pain points and unmet needs.
5. Research: Conduct thorough research on the customer's industry, business, and competitors. This background knowledge enables you to ask informed questions and understand their context.
6. Patience: Allow the customer to express themselves fully. Avoid rushing through the conversation or jumping to conclusions prematurely.

Uncovering Customer Needs and Pain Points Across the Sales Cycle

Uncovering customer needs and pain points is not confined to a single phase of the sales cycle; it's a continuous process that spans the entire journey:

1. Uncovering Needs and Pain Points in Prospecting: In the prospecting phase, uncovering needs and pain points helps you determine whether the customer is a viable prospect and whether your offerings align with their challenges.
2. Uncovering Needs and Pain Points in Needs Analysis: During the discovery phase, your focus is on delving deep to understand the customer's underlying challenges, objectives, and motivations.
3. Uncovering Needs and Pain Points in Presentation: In the presentation phase, your insights into customer needs and

pain points allow you to tailor your pitch to address their specific concerns and priorities.
4. Uncovering Needs and Pain Points in Handling Objections: Effective objection handling hinges on your understanding of the customer's pain points. By addressing objections proactively, you demonstrate your commitment to solving their problems.
5. Uncovering Needs and Pain Points in Closing: In the closing phase, your ability to revisit and align your solution with the customer's needs can provide the final push toward a successful deal.
6. Uncovering Needs and Pain Points in Post-Sale Support: Even after the sale, your efforts to uncover and address the customer's evolving needs and pain points are crucial for maintaining a strong relationship.

Leveraging Uncovering Customer Needs and Pain Points for Success

Uncovering customer needs and pain points is not just a task; it's a strategic advantage that can be leveraged for greater success:

1. Building Rapport: Understanding a customer's needs and pain points fosters rapport. It shows that you are genuinely interested in their well-being and committed to addressing their concerns.
2. Tailoring Solutions: Armed with insights into a customer's needs and pain points, you can tailor your solutions to align perfectly with their objectives. This customization enhances the perceived value of your offerings.

3. Overcoming Objections: Knowing a customer's pain points equips you to anticipate objections and address them proactively. It demonstrates your expertise and problem-solving abilities.
4. Establishing Trust: Customers are more likely to trust a sales professional who takes the time to understand their unique challenges. Trust is the bedrock of successful negotiations.
5. Effective Communication: Uncovering needs and pain points leads to more effective communication. Your messages become relevant, resonant, and solution-oriented.

In the grand narrative of sales, "Uncovering Customer Needs and Pain Points" is the area where sales professionals become detectives of desire and architects of solutions. It's where you move beyond the surface to unveil the core challenges and aspirations that drive decisions. It's not just about asking questions; it's about asking the right questions that lead to profound insights. In a world where superficial interactions abound, uncovering customer needs and pain points is the art of depth and understanding. It's not just a skill; it's the foundation of effective sales and the pathway to successful outcomes in the realm of sales negotiation.

Demonstrating Empathy: The Bedrock of Customer-Centric Sales

In the realm of sales negotiation, the ability to demonstrate empathy emerges as a pivotal skill that transcends mere transactions, forging authentic connections with customers and enhancing the likelihood of successful outcomes. This chapter delves into the profound significance of demonstrating empathy, emphasizing its pivotal role in building trust, understanding customer needs, and navigating complex negotiations.

The Significance of Demonstrating Empathy

Demonstrating Empathy is more than a courtesy; it is the cornerstone upon which customer-centric sales are built. Here's why demonstrating empathy holds such paramount importance:

1. Building Trust: Empathy fosters trust and rapport between sales professionals and customers. It shows that you genuinely care about the customer's well-being and are not solely focused on making a sale.
2. Understanding Customer Needs: Empathetic listening and responses enable you to gain deeper insight into customer needs and pain points. This understanding guides your recommendations and solutions.
3. Effective Communication: Empathy enhances communication by allowing you to connect with customers on an emotional level. It paves the way for open, honest, and transparent dialogue.
4. Conflict Resolution: In cases of objections or conflicts, empathy can defuse tension and create an atmosphere conducive to finding mutually agreeable solutions.
5. Customer Loyalty: Customers who feel understood and valued are more likely to remain loyal and provide repeat business. Demonstrating empathy is the pathway to building long-term relationships.

The Building Blocks of Demonstrating Empathy

Empathy is not an inherent trait; it is a skill that can be honed through practice and conscious effort. Building the ability to demonstrate empathy involves consistent demonstration of these essential building blocks:

1. Active Listening: Active listening is at the heart of empathy. Pay full attention to the customer, minimizing distractions and focusing on what they are saying, both verbally and nonverbally.
2. Perspective-Taking: Try to see the situation from the customer's perspective. Understand their emotions, concerns, and objectives as if you were in their shoes.
3. Open-Mindedness: Approach each customer interaction with an open mind, free of judgment or preconceived notions. Be receptive to their thoughts and feelings.
4. Reflective Responses: Respond to the customer's statements with empathy and understanding. Acknowledge their feelings and concerns, demonstrating that you've heard them.
5. Patience: Be patient and allow the customer to express themselves fully. Avoid rushing through the conversation or interrupting prematurely.
6. Nonverbal Communication: Pay attention to your own nonverbal cues, such as body language, facial expressions, and tone of voice. These can convey empathy or its absence.

Demonstrating Empathy Across the Sales Cycle

Demonstrating empathy is not limited to one phase of the sales cycle; it is an ongoing practice that spans the entire journey:

1. Demonstrating Empathy in Prospecting: In the prospecting phase, demonstrating empathy involves understanding the prospect's situation and challenges, even before the formal conversation begins.
2. Demonstrating Empathy in Needs Analysis: During the discovery phase, empathy is crucial. It allows you to delve deep into the customer's underlying challenges, aspirations, and motivations.
3. Demonstrating Empathy in Presentation: In the presentation phase, empathy enables you to tailor your pitch to address the specific needs and concerns you've identified.
4. Demonstrating Empathy in Handling Objections: When objections arise, empathy can soften the impact and pave the way for productive objection handling. It shows that you care about resolving concerns.
5. Demonstrating Empathy in Closing: In the closing phase, demonstrating empathy reassures the customer that their needs and concerns are your priority, facilitating a confident decision.
6. Demonstrating Empathy in Post-Sale Support: Even after the sale, demonstrating empathy remains essential. It shows that you continue to care about the customer's well-being and are dedicated to their success.

Leveraging Demonstrating Empathy for Success

Demonstrating empathy is not just a gesture; it is a strategic advantage that can be leveraged for greater success:

1. Building Trust: Empathy fosters trust and rapport, laying a solid foundation for successful negotiations. Customers are

more likely to trust a sales professional who genuinely cares about their well-being.
2. Understanding Customer Needs: Empathy allows you to gain deeper insight into customer needs and pain points. This understanding guides your recommendations and solutions, making them more relevant and impactful.
3. Effective Communication: Empathy enhances communication by creating a connection on an emotional level. It paves the way for open, honest, and transparent dialogue.
4. Conflict Resolution: In cases of objections or conflicts, empathy can defuse tension and create an atmosphere conducive to finding mutually agreeable solutions.
5. Customer Loyalty: Customers who feel understood and valued are more likely to remain loyal and provide repeat business. Demonstrating empathy is the pathway to building long-term relationships.

Demonstrating Empathy is the domain where sales professionals transition from transactional agents to trusted advisors. It's where you move beyond scripts and pitches to connect on a human level. It's not just about what you say; it's about how you make the customer feel. In a world inundated with sales pitches, demonstrating empathy is the authentic resonance that sets you apart and paves the way for successful outcomes in the realm of sales negotiation. It's not just a skill; it's the bedrock of customer-centric sales.

CHAPTER 5

NEGOTIATION STRATEGIES

*I*n the dynamic world of sales, negotiation is the linchpin that bridges the gap between prospects' needs and the value propositions offered by sales professionals. The art of negotiation in sales goes beyond closing deals; it's about fostering trust, understanding customer desires, and creating mutually beneficial agreements. This chapter delves into the specialized domain of negotiation strategies in sales, where the delicate interplay of persuasion, empathy, and strategy takes center stage. Here, you'll discover the tactics, insights, and principles that empower sales negotiators to navigate the complex terrain of client interactions, transforming leads into loyal customers and challenges into opportunities for growth.

Win-Win vs. Win-Lose Approaches: Shaping the Dynamics of Negotiation

Negotiation is an intricate interplay of strategies and tactics, with outcomes ranging from cooperative wins to competitive battles. In Chapter 5, we explore the fundamental concepts of win-win and win-lose approaches, which serve as the foundation for shaping the dynamics of negotiation.

The Win-Win Approach: Creating Value Together

"Win-win negotiation" embodies a collaborative mindset where the primary objective is to create value for all parties involved. In this approach, negotiators view the negotiation as an opportunity to satisfy everyone's interests rather than a zero-sum game where one party's gain is another's loss. Here's a closer look at the key elements of the win-win approach:

1. Cooperation: Win-win negotiations emphasize cooperation over competition. The parties work together to identify common interests and shared goals.
2. Value Creation: The focus is on generating value, not merely distributing it. Negotiators explore options and solutions that maximize benefits for all parties.
3. Open Communication: Effective communication is essential in Win-Win negotiations. Parties openly share information, concerns, and priorities, fostering an environment of trust and transparency.
4. Problem-Solving: Win-win negotiators approach challenges as mutual problems to solve. They seek innovative solutions that address everyone's needs.

5. Long-Term Relationships: Building and maintaining long-term relationships is a core tenet of the Win-win approach. It recognizes that today's negotiation partners may be tomorrow's collaborators.
6. Mutual Satisfaction: Success in Win-wWin negotiations is measured by the mutual satisfaction of all parties. It's not about one side winning and the other losing; it's about everyone walking away feeling that their interests were met.

The Win-win approach is particularly effective in sales negotiations, where the goal is to establish trust, build relationships, and secure repeat business. By prioritizing customer satisfaction and seeking solutions that align with their needs, sales professionals can create lasting partnerships that benefit both parties.

#The Win-Lose Approach: Zero-Sum Competition

Conversely, the Win-lose approach embodies a competitive mindset, often associated with distributive or adversarial negotiation. In win-lose negotiations, one party's gain is perceived as another's loss, and the goal is to secure the best possible outcome for oneself, often at the expense of the other party. Key characteristics of the Win-Lose approach include:

1. Competition: Win-lose negotiations are marked by competition and a "winner takes all" mentality. Each party strives to maximize their share of the pie.
2. Fixed Resources: It often assumes that resources are fixed, leading to a limited pool of benefits to be distributed. This can result in a confrontational atmosphere.

3. Tactical Maneuvering: Win-lose negotiators employ tactics and strategies to gain an advantage, sometimes resorting to deception or coercion.
4. Short-Term Focus: The focus is on immediate gains, even if it comes at the expense of long-term relationships. Parties may prioritize short-term wins over future collaboration.
5. Zero-Sum Mindset: Win-lose negotiators view negotiation as a zero-sum game, where one party's gain equals the other's loss. This can lead to hostility and mistrust.

While the Win-lose approach may be effective in certain situations, such as competitive bidding scenarios, it often falls short in sales negotiations. Aggressive tactics and short-term gains can damage relationships, tarnish a company's reputation, and deter repeat business. Sales professionals who prioritize Win-win approaches tend to build stronger, more enduring client relationships, ultimately leading to sustained success.

Choosing the Right Approach

The choice between a win-win and win-lose approach depends on the context of the negotiation, the parties involved, and the desired outcomes. Here are factors to consider when deciding which approach to adopt:

1. Relationship Importance: If the negotiation involves parties with whom you wish to establish long-term relationships, a win-win approach is generally more suitable. Prioritizing collaboration and mutual satisfaction can lay the foundation for enduring partnerships.

2. Complex Issues: In negotiations where the issues are multifaceted and require creative solutions, a win-win approach can unlock innovative ways to address challenges and create value.
3. Reputational Concerns: Sales professionals should be mindful of their company's reputation. Adopting a win-lose approach that appears exploitative or aggressive can damage the brand and deter potential customers.
4. Power Dynamics: Consider the relative power of the parties involved. In situations where one party holds a significant advantage, they may be tempted to pursue a win-lose approach. However, this can lead to resentment and strained relationships.
5. Negotiation Style: Personal negotiation styles also play a role. Some individuals naturally lean toward cooperation and collaboration (win-win), while others may default to a more competitive stance (win-lose).
6. Cultural Considerations: Cultural norms and expectations can influence negotiation approaches. In some cultures, a collaborative approach is the norm, while in others, competitive tactics may be expected.
7. Time Sensitivity: Urgency and time constraints can impact the chosen approach. In time-sensitive situations, parties may be more inclined to adopt a win-lose approach to quickly reach a resolution.
8. Goal Alignment: Assess whether the goals and interests of the parties are aligned or divergent. When common ground exists, a win-win approach is often more productive.

Navigating the Hybrid Approach

In practice, negotiation often involves elements of both win-win and win-lose strategies, creating a hybrid approach. This hybrid approach, sometimes referred to as "coopetition," acknowledges that negotiation dynamics are rarely black and white. Negotiators may collaborate on certain issues while competing with others, seeking a balanced outcome.

Sales professionals often navigate this hybrid terrain, striving to satisfy customer needs while also achieving their sales targets. This requires the agility to adapt the approach based on the specific situation and the evolving dynamics of the negotiation.

This specific portion underscores the pivotal role of negotiation strategies in shaping the outcomes of sales negotiations. Whether one chooses to adopt a win-win or win-lose approach—or navigate the intricate terrain of a hybrid strategy—depends on a multitude of factors. In the world of sales, where relationships, reputation, and long-term success are paramount, the win-win approach tends to be the preferred path. Prioritizing collaboration, understanding customer needs, and fostering trust are the hallmarks of successful sales negotiations, where the goal is not merely to win but to win together, creating enduring value for all parties involved.

Principled Negotiation (Getting to Yes): The Art of Agreement

Negotiation is an intricate balance of dialogue and emotions, where disparate interests converge and diverge and where the skillful navigation of conflicts can lead to mutually beneficial agreements. In this chapter, we delve into the concept of "principled negotiation as popularized by the seminal work *Getting to Yes* by Roger Fisher and William Ury. Principled negotiation represents a strategic framework that transcends traditional win-lose scenarios, focusing on collaborative problem-solving and principled decision-making. It offers a powerful blueprint for negotiators seeking not only to reach agreements but to do so in a way that preserves relationships and generates sustainable outcomes.

The Rules of Principled Negotiation

At the heart of principled negotiation lie four foundational principles that guide the negotiation process:

1. Separate People From the Problem: The first principle emphasizes the importance of separating people from the problem. In any negotiation, there are two elements at play: the substantive issues and the interpersonal dynamics. Principled negotiation urges negotiators to address the issues while recognizing that people often have emotional investments in those issues. By acknowledging and addressing emotions, rather than allowing them to derail the negotiation, parties can work more effectively toward a solution.
2. Focus on Interests, Not Positions: The second principle encourages negotiators to focus on interests, not positions. People tend to adopt fixed positions in negotiations, often in opposition to one another. Instead of clinging to rigid positions, principled negotiation suggests that negotiators should uncover and understand the underlying interests that drive those positions. Identifying shared interests provides a

foundation for creative problem-solving and the generation of mutually beneficial solutions.
3. Invent Options for Mutual Gain: The third principle advocates for the "invention of options for mutual gain." Rather than settling for a single, predetermined solution, principled negotiation encourages parties to explore a range of creative alternatives. This approach expands the possibilities for achieving outcomes that meet the interests of both parties, often resulting in solutions that exceed initial expectations.
4. Insist on Using Objective Criteria: The fourth principle calls for the use of "objective criteria" to assess proposed solutions. Objective criteria provide an unbiased standard against which potential agreements can be evaluated. Instead of relying solely on subjective judgments or power dynamics, negotiators can refer to these external standards to determine the fairness and legitimacy of proposed solutions.

Benefits of Principled Negotiation in Sales

Principled negotiation offers several distinct advantages in sales negotiations:

1. Relationship Building: By focusing on understanding the customer's interests and seeking mutually beneficial solutions, sales professionals can strengthen customer relationships. This approach can lead to repeat business and referrals.
2. Innovative Solutions: The emphasis on inventing options for mutual gain encourages creativity and flexibility in crafting solutions. Sales professionals can tailor their offerings to meet the unique needs of each customer better.

3. Objective Evaluation: Using objective criteria provides a transparent and fair method for evaluating proposals. Customers are more likely to accept agreements that are based on external standards rather than subjective judgments.
4. Conflict Resolution: Principled negotiation provides a structured framework for addressing conflicts and disagreements. Instead of escalating disputes, sales professionals can navigate them constructively.

Principled negotiation, as expounded in *Getting to Yes*, represents a powerful approach to negotiation that transcends traditional win-lose dynamics. Its principles of separating people from the problem, focusing on interests, inventing options for mutual gain, and insisting on objective criteria provide a roadmap for achieving agreements that satisfy the interests of all parties involved. In sales negotiations, where relationships, customer satisfaction, and long-term success are paramount, principled negotiation offers a strategic framework that aligns with the goals of building trust, understanding customer needs, and fostering collaboration. It's not just about reaching an agreement; it's about reaching the right agreement—one that benefits everyone involved.

The Power of BATNA: Unveiling Your Negotiation Safety Net

In the intricate realm of negotiation, where outcomes are uncertain and conflicts abound, having a clear understanding of your BATNA (Best Alternative to a Negotiated Agreement) can be the linchpin that empowers you to make informed decisions and secure favourable results. This part delves into the profound significance of BATNA, dissecting its components and offering insights into how it shapes the dynamics of negotiation.

What is BATNA?

BATNA, an acronym coined by Roger Fisher and William Ury in their seminal book *Getting to Yes*," refers to your best alternative to a negotiated agreement. Simply put, it represents the course of action you would pursue if the current negotiation were to fail or if you walked away from the table. Your BATNA is your safety net, your plan B, and your leverage in negotiations.

The Components of BATNA

To understand BATNA fully, it's essential to break it down into its key components:

1. Best Alternative: Your BATNA is not just any alternative; it's the best alternative available to you outside of the current negotiation. It represents the most favourable outcome you can achieve without reaching an agreement with the other party.
2. To a Negotiated Agreement: The alternative in BATNA is specific to the negotiated agreement under consideration. It's the alternative to whatever deal or arrangement is being discussed at the negotiation table.
3. Preparation: Developing a strong BATNA requires preparation and research. You need to identify and evaluate alternative options, including their potential benefits and drawbacks.

The Significance of BATNA

Understanding and leveraging your BATNA is crucial for several reasons:

1. Empowerment: Your BATNA empowers you with the confidence to walk away from a negotiation that doesn't meet your needs. This empowerment can lead to more assertive and favourable outcomes.
2. Strategic Advantage: A strong BATNA provides a strategic advantage. It enables you to negotiate from a position of strength, knowing that you have a viable alternative if the current negotiation doesn't yield the desired results.
3. Risk Mitigation: BATNA serves as a risk mitigation tool. It reduces the pressure to agree to unfavourable terms out of fear of not reaching a deal.
4. Informed Decision-Making: When you have a clear understanding of your BATNA, you can make informed decisions about whether to accept an offer, continue negotiating, or walk away.
5. Flexibility: BATNA allows for flexibility in negotiations. It gives you the freedom to explore different options and potentially craft more creative and advantageous agreements.

Developing Your BATNA

Developing a robust BATNA involves a series of steps:

1. Identify Alternatives: Begin by identifying all possible alternatives to the negotiated agreement. What other courses of action are available to you if the current negotiation doesn't pan out?

2. Evaluate Alternatives: Once you've identified potential alternatives, evaluate them rigorously. Consider factors such as feasibility, benefits, risks, and costs associated with each alternative.
3. Rank Alternatives: After evaluating the alternatives, rank them in order of desirability. Your BATNA should be the most favorable alternative among the options.
4. Assess BATNA Strength: Assess the strength of your BATNA by examining how it compares to the negotiated agreement's terms and benefits. A strong BATNA is one that offers outcomes equal to or better than the current negotiation.
5. Improve Your BATNA: In some cases, it may be possible to enhance your BATNA through further research, preparation, or negotiations with third parties.

The Role of BATNA in Negotiations

BATNA plays a pivotal role in negotiations, influencing your approach, strategy, and decisions:

1. Determination of Reservation Point: Your BATNA helps you establish your reservation point—the point at which you would be indifferent between accepting an offer and pursuing your BATNA. Knowing your reservation point guides your acceptance or rejection of offers during negotiations.
2. Setting Aspirations: BATNA also influences your aspiration point—the ideal outcome you hope to achieve in the negotiation. Your aspiration point is anchored by the strength of your BATNA. If your BATNA is strong, your aspirations may be higher.

3. Negotiation Strategy: Armed with the knowledge of your BATNA, you can adopt different negotiation strategies. For instance, if your BATNA is weak, you may adopt a more cooperative approach to reach an agreement. Conversely, a strong BATNA may lead to a more competitive stance.
4. Walk-Away Point: Your BATNA defines your walk-away point—the point at which you are willing to abandon the negotiation and pursue your alternative. Knowing this point helps you avoid agreeing to unfavourable terms out of desperation.
5. Leverage and Power: A strong BATNA enhances your leverage and power in negotiations. It signals to the other party that you have viable alternatives and are not beholden to a particular deal. This can influence their willingness to make concessions.

BATNA in Sales Negotiation

In sales negotiation, understanding and leveraging BATNA is particularly critical due to the potential for long-term relationships and the competitive nature of the industry. Here's how BATNA applies in sales:

1. Understanding Customer BATNA: Effective sales professionals not only develop their own BATNA but also seek to understand the customer's BATNA. This insight can help tailor offers and negotiations to align with the customer's needs and alternatives.
2. Preserving Relationships: A strong focus on BATNA can prevent sales professionals from

pushing customers too hard or attempting to secure deals that are unfavourable to both parties. This focus on mutual benefit can help build trust and long-term relationships.
3. Negotiation Agility: Sales professionals with a clear understanding of their BATNA can be more agile in negotiations. They can pivot to different strategies based on the perceived strength of their BATNA and the customer's priorities.
4. Risk Mitigation: BATNA serves as a risk mitigation tool in sales. Sales professionals are less likely to make concessions that could harm their organization's interests or reputation.

In the delicate process of negotiation, BATNA emerges as a guiding light that illuminates your path empowers your decisions, and shapes the dynamics of the negotiation. By understanding and leveraging your best alternative to a negotiated agreement, you position yourself for success, whether in sales, business transactions, or personal interactions. BATNA offers not only a safety net but a strategic advantage—a tool that transforms negotiation from a gamble into a calculated endeavour, where informed choices lead to outcomes that align with your interests and objectives.

Creating Value in Negotiation: The Art of Expanding the Pie

Negotiation is often perceived as a zero-sum game, where one party's gain is seen as another's loss. However, the most skilled negotiators understand that the true art of negotiation lies in creating value—in finding ways to expand the pie so all parties can benefit. This chapter unravels the principles and strategies behind value creation in negotiation, emphasizing its role in fostering cooperation, building relationships, and securing mutually advantageous agreements.

The Zero-Sum vs. Value Creation Dilemma

In traditional negotiations, the prevailing belief is that there's a fixed amount of value to be divided among the parties, and the goal is to secure as large a piece of that fixed pie as possible. This perspective often leads to competitive, win-lose dynamics where concessions are viewed as sacrifices, and each gain by one party is perceived as a loss for the other.

However, this zero-sum mindset can be limiting. It overlooks the possibility of "value creation," where negotiators actively work to increase the overall value available, thereby benefiting all parties involved. The shift from a zero-sum approach to value creation marks a fundamental change in negotiation philosophy—one that can lead to more favourable outcomes, better relationships, and a win-win mindset.

The Principles of Value Creation

Value creation in negotiation is underpinned by several core principles:

1. Interest-Based Negotiation: Value creation aligns with the interest-based approach to negotiation. Rather than fixating on positions or demands, negotiators focus on identifying and satisfying the underlying interests and needs of all parties. This approach opens the door to creative problem-solving.

2. Expanding the Pie: Value creation involves finding ways to expand the size of the pie—that is, increasing the overall value available for distribution. This can be achieved through innovative solutions, additional resources, or by uncovering previously overlooked opportunities.
3. Joint Gain: The goal of value creation is to achieve joint gain, where all parties benefit more than they would in a strictly distributive, win-lose negotiation. It promotes cooperation and collaboration over competition.
4. Focus on Long-Term Relationships: Value creation is closely tied to relationship-building. It recognizes that successful negotiations can pave the way for ongoing partnerships and collaborations, making it essential for maintaining trust and goodwill.

Strategies for Value Creation

Creating value in negotiation requires a strategic approach that goes beyond traditional haggling. Here are some key strategies to foster value creation:

1. Information Sharing: Open and transparent communication is vital. Sharing information about needs, priorities, and constraints can uncover opportunities for value creation.
2. Joint Problem-Solving: Encourage collaborative problem-solving. Parties should work together to identify common challenges and explore creative solutions that benefit all.
3. Expanding the Scope: Consider expanding the scope of the negotiation beyond the initial issues. Are there additional areas of mutual interest that can be explored to create value?

4. Innovation: Embrace innovative thinking. Look for unconventional solutions and approaches that can enhance the overall value of the negotiation.
5. Trade-offs: Be open to trade-offs. Value creation often involves making concessions on certain issues to gain advantages over others.
6. Value Metrics: Develop metrics for assessing value. What criteria can be used to determine whether a potential agreement creates more value than the status quo?

Value Creation in Sales Negotiation

In sales negotiation, value creation takes on particular significance. Sales professionals are not merely focused on closing deals but also on building long-term customer relationships and securing repeat business. Here's how value creation applies in sales negotiation:

1. Understanding Customer Needs: Sales professionals must thoroughly understand the customer's needs and priorities. This knowledge allows for the tailoring of solutions that create value by addressing specific pain points.
2. Offering Customization: Value is often created through customization. Sales professionals can explore how their offerings can be tailored to better align with the customer's requirements.
3. Creating Win-Win Agreements: In sales, value creation is exemplified through win-win agreements. Both the seller and the customer should perceive the agreement as delivering more value than they would have achieved without it.
4. Upselling and Cross-Selling: Value can be expanded by identifying additional products or services that complement

the customer's purchase, adding value without significantly increasing costs.
5. Long-Term Partnerships: Sales professionals should prioritize long-term partnerships over short-term gains. By consistently delivering value and meeting customer needs, they can secure customer loyalty and repeat business.

Building Trust and Rapport

Value creation in negotiation is intimately connected to the establishment of trust and rapport. When parties believe that the negotiation process is fair, transparent, and focused on mutual benefit, trust is nurtured. Trust, in turn, fosters an environment where value creation can thrive.

The Role of BATNA in Value Creation

BATNA (Best Alternative to a Negotiated Agreement), as discussed earlier, plays a crucial role in value creation. A strong BATNA provides negotiators with the confidence and leverage needed to pursue value-creating solutions. When negotiators know they have a viable alternative, they are more inclined to explore creative and mutually beneficial agreements, as they are not solely dependent on the current negotiation for their desired outcome.

Value creation in negotiation is a paradigm shift from the zero-sum mentality. It embodies the idea that negotiation is not just about dividing a fixed pie but about expanding that pie for the benefit of all parties involved. In sales negotiation, this approach is particularly potent, as it aligns with the objectives of building trust, fostering long-term relationships, and securing customer loyalty. Value creation is the essence of win-win negotiation, where both sides walk away feeling that they have not only achieved their goals but also enhanced the overall value of the deal. By embracing this philosophy, negotiators unlock the true potential of negotiation, transforming conflicts into opportunities and adversarial encounters into collaborative partnerships.

CHAPTER 6

HANDLING OBJECTIONS AND PUSHBACK

*I*n the dynamic world of sales, objections and pushback are not roadblocks but opportunities. This chapter delves into the art of effectively handling objections and pushback in sales—a vital skill that separates successful sales professionals from the rest. Here, we explore proven strategies and techniques to turn objections into bridges, address concerns with finesse, and, ultimately, transform resistance into customer buy-in. In this journey, we uncover the power of active listening, empathetic responses, and persuasive communication, equipping you with the tools to navigate objections, strengthen client relationships, and close deals with confidence.

Identifying Common Objections in Sales: Anticipating and Overcoming Challenges

Sales, often described as a delicate exchange of words and emotion between buyer and seller, is fraught with moments of resistance and skepticism. Objections are a natural part of this process, reflecting the buyer's concerns, questions, or hesitations. This portion sheds light on the most common objections encountered in sales, exploring their underlying causes, and equipping sales professionals with strategies to effectively navigate and overcome these hurdles.

The Nature of Sales Objections

Objections in sales are essentially expressions of doubt or hesitation from the buyer's perspective. They can take various forms, including questions, concerns, or outright rejections. It's crucial to recognize that objections are not necessarily barriers to closing a deal; instead, they are opportunities for clarification and persuasion.

Reason for Objections

Understanding the reasons behind objections is essential to address them effectively. Common reasons for objections include:

1. Lack of Information: Buyers may object due to insufficient information or misunderstanding about the product or service being offered.
2. Risk Aversion: Fear of making a wrong decision or the risk associated with the purchase can lead to objections.

3. Price Concerns: Price objections are prevalent, as buyers often seek the best return for their investment.
4. Competing Priorities: Buyers may have competing priorities or limited budgets that lead to objections.
5. Trust and Credibility: Trust in the seller's integrity and the credibility of the product or service can influence objections.
6. Decision-Making Process: Objections can also arise when buyers are uncertain about their own decision-making process or when multiple stakeholders are involved.

Common Sales Objections

While objections can vary based on industry, product, or service, some objections tend to be recurrent in many sales scenarios. Here are common objections sales professionals often encounter:

1. Price Objection: "It's too expensive." Price objections are ubiquitous, and they often reflect the need for further justification of the product's value.
2. Timing Objection: "It's not the right time." Buyers may object due to concerns about timing, often linked to budgetary constraints or other priorities.
3. Competition Objection: "I have a better offer from your competitor." Buyers may compare offerings from different providers, presenting a challenge to demonstrate superior value.
4. Product Knowledge Objection: "I need more information." A lack of understanding about the product or service can lead to objections rooted in the need for more information.

5. Trust Objection: "I'm not sure I can trust your company." Trust objections require building credibility and addressing concerns about reliability and integrity.
6. Need Objection: "I don't see how this meets my needs." Buyers may object when they don't perceive a clear alignment between their needs and the offering.
7. Authority Objection: "I need to check with my manager." Objections related to decision-making authority often require involving multiple stakeholders.
8. Fear Objection: "I'm afraid of the risks involved." Fear-based objections stem from concerns about potential negative consequences or risks associated with the purchase.

Anticipating and Preparing for Objections

Proactive preparation is key to effectively handling objections. Sales professionals can employ several strategies to anticipate objections and develop tailored responses:

1. Market Research: Comprehensive market research helps identify common objections within a specific industry or product category.
2. Customer Profiling: Understanding the buyer persona enables sales professionals to anticipate objections specific to that audience.
3. Sales Training: Ongoing training equips sales teams with objection-handling techniques and strategies.
4. Feedback Loop: Collecting feedback from sales representatives about objections encountered in the field can inform objection-handling strategies.

Overcoming Common Sales Objections

Addressing objections effectively requires a combination of active listening, empathy, and persuasive communication. Here are strategies to overcome common objections:

1. Price Objection:
   - Value Communication: Emphasize the value and benefits the product or service offers relative to its price.
   - Payment Options: Offer flexible payment plans or financing options to ease budgetary concerns.
   - Comparative Analysis: Provide data or comparisons demonstrating cost savings or advantages over competitors.

2. Timing Objection:
   - Assess Urgency: Understand the buyer's timeline and assess whether there are genuine constraints.
   - Create Urgency: Highlight the immediate benefits of your offering and the potential consequences of delaying.

3. Competition Objection:
   - Unique Selling Proposition (USP): Emphasize the unique features or advantages that set your offering apart from competitors.
   - Customer Testimonials: Share success stories and testimonials from satisfied customers who chose your product over competitors'.

4. Product Knowledge Objection:
   - Educate Effectively: Provide clear and concise information that addresses the buyer's questions and concerns.

- Demo and Samples: Offer product demonstrations or samples to showcase its value first-hand.

5. Trust Objection:
   - Build Credibility: Share credentials, certifications, or industry awards that demonstrate your company's reliability.
   - Testimonials and References: Offer references or case studies that illustrate positive experiences with your company.

6. Need Objection:
   - Consultative Approach: Engage in a consultative conversation to understand the buyer's specific needs and tailor your offering accordingly.
   - Problem-Solving: Showcase how your product or service addresses the buyer's pain points and meets their unique requirements.

7. Authority Objection:
   - Stakeholder Involvement: Facilitate conversations with key decision-makers to address concerns and obtain buy-in.

8. Fear Objection:
   - Risk Mitigation: Address potential risks by providing warranties, guarantees, or risk-reduction strategies.
   - Customer Success Stories: Share examples of how your product or service has successfully mitigated similar concerns for other customers.

Role of Active Listening

Active listening is a foundational skill in handling objections. Sales professionals should actively listen to the buyer's concerns, ask clarifying questions, and acknowledge their perspective. By demonstrating genuine interest and empathy, sales professionals can build rapport and trust, making objection resolution more effective.

The Win-Win Approach

A successful objection-handling approach seeks not only to address the buyer's concerns but also to find mutually beneficial solutions. The goal is not to "win" the argument but to collaboratively reach an agreement that satisfies both parties.

Objections in sales are not hurdles but stepping stones to successful deals. Identifying common objections, understanding their underlying causes, and proactively preparing to address them equips sales professionals with the tools to navigate objections effectively. By employing active listening, empathy, and persuasive communication, sales professionals can transform objections into opportunities for clarification, persuasion, and, ultimately, successful sales closures. Handling objections is not just a skill; it's an art that fosters trust, builds relationships, and leads to win-win outcomes in the dynamic world of sales.

Responding Effectively to Objections: Turning Challenges into Opportunities

In the world of sales, objections are not stumbling blocks; they are invitations to engage, clarify, and persuade. This portion delves into the art of responding effectively to objections, understanding that objections are not merely hurdles but opportunities for building trust, addressing concerns, and, ultimately, securing the sale. Here, we explore the strategies, techniques, and mindset required to navigate objections with finesse and achieve mutually beneficial outcomes.

The Nature of Sales Objections

Sales objections are a natural part of the sales process, representing the buyer's reservations, questions, or hesitations. Rather than viewing objections as barriers, sales professionals should see them as valuable insights into the buyer's thought process and an opportunity to engage in meaningful dialogue.

The Anatomy of an Effective Response

An effective response to objections is built on several key principles:

1. Active Listening: Start by actively listening to the objection. Pay attention to the buyer's words, tone, and underlying concerns. This demonstrates respect and genuine interest.
2. Empathy: Put yourself in the buyer's shoes to understand their perspective and emotions. Empathy builds rapport and trust.
3. Clarification: Seek clarification if the objection is not entirely clear. Ask open-ended questions to uncover the specific concern.
4. Acknowledgment: Acknowledge the buyer's objection without dismissing it. Validating their perspective fosters a collaborative atmosphere.
5. Information and Education: Provide relevant information and education to address the objection. Be concise and clear in your explanations.

6. Benefit Highlighting: Emphasize the benefits and value of your product or service in relation to the objection. Explain how it addresses the buyer's needs.
7. Storytelling: Share relevant success stories or case studies to illustrate how others have benefited from your offering in similar situations.
8. Alternative Solutions: If applicable, present alternative solutions or options that accommodate the buyer's concerns.
9. Trial Close: After responding to the objection, use a trial close to gauge the buyer's receptiveness. For example, you can ask, "Does this address your concerns?"

Strategies for Effective Objection Handling

Navigating objections effectively requires a strategic approach. Here are strategies that sales professionals can employ:

1. Preparation: Anticipate common objections based on market research and customer profiling. Develop objection-handling responses in advance.
2. Scripted Responses vs. Customization: While having scripted objection-handling responses can be helpful, tailor your responses to the specific objection and the buyer's unique circumstances.
3. Overcoming Price Objections:
    - Value Emphasis: Reiterate the value and benefits your product or service offers, emphasizing its worth.
    - Payment Options: Present flexible payment plans or financing options to ease budget concerns.
    - Value-Added Extras: Highlight any additional features, services, or bonuses that come with the purchase.

4. Addressing Timing Objections:
   - Urgency Explanation: Reveal the advantages of taking action promptly, explaining the potential benefits of not delaying.
   - Offer Trials or Demos: Suggest trial periods or product demos to showcase immediate benefits.

5. Handling Competition Objections:
   - Competitive Advantages: Reiterate the unique selling points that set your offering apart from your competitors'.
   - Customer Testimonials: Share testimonials from satisfied customers who chose your product over competitors'.

6. Dealing with Trust Objections:
   - Credibility Demonstration: Share credentials, certifications, or industry awards that affirm your company's reliability.
   - Trust-Building Steps: Offer to provide references, customer reviews, or case studies to establish trust.

7. Responding to Product Knowledge Objections:
   - Educational Approach: Provide clear and concise explanations, using simple language to enhance understanding.
   - Visual Aids: Utilize visuals or product demonstrations to illustrate key points.

8. Tackling Need Objections:
   - Consultative Engagement: Engage in a consultative conversation to uncover the buyer's specific needs and adapt your offering accordingly.

- Problem-Solving: Showcase how your product or service addresses the buyer's pain points and meets their unique requirements.

The Art of Handling Emotional Objections

In sales, objections can be emotionally charged. Buyers may express fear, skepticism, or frustration. Effective objection handling also entails addressing these emotional objections:

1. Empathy: Acknowledge the buyer's emotions with empathy. For example, you can say, "I understand that this decision can be challenging."
2. Validation: Validate the buyer's feelings, even if you don't agree with their perspective. Validating emotions can de-escalate tension.
3. Reassurance: Offer reassurance by emphasizing that you are there to support them and address their concerns.
4. Storytelling: Share stories of other customers who initially had similar reservations but ultimately found value and satisfaction in your product or service.

The Win-Win Approach

An effective objection-handling approach aims for a win-win outcome. It recognizes that both the buyer and the seller should feel that they have gained something from the interaction. Seek solutions that accommodate the buyer's concerns while still aligning with your sales goals.

Handling Multiple Objections

In some cases, buyers may raise multiple objections in a single interaction. To address multiple objections effectively:

1. Prioritization: Identify the most significant objections and address them first. Start with the objections that, if resolved, are likely to lead to a successful sale.
2. Organization: Structure your responses clearly and concisely, ensuring that the buyer can follow your explanation.
3. Reconfirmation: After addressing objections, reconfirm the buyer's interest and readiness to proceed.

The Role of Follow-Up

Not all the objections can be resolved immediately. Some may require additional information, consideration, or time on the buyer's part. In such cases, commit to timely follow-up, providing the requested information or addressing outstanding concerns.

The Power of Practice

Effective objection handling is a skill that improves with practice. Sales professionals can benefit from role-playing objection scenarios during training sessions to hone their response strategies.

Responding effectively to objections is not a mere skill; it's an art that requires active listening, empathy, and persuasive communication. Objections are not barriers to a sale but stepping stones to understanding the buyer's needs and concerns. By mastering the techniques and strategies outlined in this segment, sales professionals can navigate objections with finesse, build trust, and ultimately achieve successful sales outcomes that benefit both buyer and seller. In the dynamic world of sales, objections are not challenges to be feared; they are opportunities to be embraced and conquered.

CHAPTER 7

PRICE NEGOTIATION

$\mathcal{P}$rice Negotiation is a critical juncture in the world of sales negotiation, where value, costs, and customer expectations converge. Here, we delve into the strategies, tactics, and psychology of negotiating prices effectively, understanding that price discussions can be both a challenge and an opportunity. From setting the stage for pricing discussions to employing techniques that create win-win outcomes, this chapter equips sales professionals with the knowledge and skills needed to navigate the intricacies of price negotiation. Whether it's anchoring, bundling, or using price justifications, this chapter provides a comprehensive guide to mastering the art of price negotiation in sales.

Pricing is not just about putting a number on your product or service; it's a multifaceted aspect of sales negotiation that can make or break a deal. In this chapter, we will explore various pricing strategies, each with its unique set of principles, applications, and real-world examples that will keep you engaged.

Pricing Strategies: Beyond Numbers

Pricing is one of the most dynamic and versatile components of sales negotiation. It can influence buyer decisions, shape perceptions, and directly impact the bottom line. Effective pricing strategies not only maximize revenue but also create value for both buyers and sellers. Let's embark on a journey through the fascinating landscape of pricing strategies.

1. Value-Based Pricing

    Value-based pricing is a strategy that sets prices based on the perceived value a product or service offers to customers. The key here is understanding what the customer is willing to pay for the benefits received. Imagine you are selling a high-end smartphone with advanced camera features. By positioning it as the best tool for capturing life's moments, you can justify a premium price, appealing to photography enthusiasts who value exceptional image quality.

2. Penetration Pricing

    Penetration pricing involves setting an initially low price to gain a foothold in a competitive market. Once you've captured a significant market share and established brand loyalty, you can gradually increase prices. Consider the example of Amazon's entry into the e-reader market with the Kindle. Amazon priced the device aggressively to encourage rapid adoption, eventually making profits from e-book sales and Kindle-related services.

3. Premium Pricing

    Premium pricing is the strategy of setting prices at a premium to convey exclusivity, luxury, or exceptional quality. Brands like Rolex and Louis Vuitton excel in this approach. By positioning their products as elite, they attract a niche market willing to pay a premium for the prestige associated with owning these items.

4. Dynamic Pricing

   Dynamic pricing involves adjusting prices in real-time based on various factors such as demand, supply, competitor pricing, and customer behaviour. Airlines are masters of dynamic pricing. They change ticket prices based on factors like the time of booking, seat availability, and even the user's browsing history to maximize revenue.

5. Loss Leader Pricing

   This strategy involves selling a product below cost or at a minimal profit margin to attract customers. Supermarkets often use this approach to entice shoppers. For instance, a store might sell a popular soft drink at a loss to get customers through the door, expecting them to buy other items with higher profit margins during their visit.

6. Bundle Pricing

   Bundle pricing combines several products or services into a single package at a lower overall price than if customers were to purchase each item individually. Software companies often use this strategy. Consider Microsoft Office, which offers a suite of applications at a lower cost than buying each application separately.

7. Psychological Pricing

   Psychological pricing plays on the psychology of consumer perception. Pricing items at $9.99 instead of $10 exploits the tendency for consumers to focus on the leftmost digit. This technique creates the illusion of a significantly lower price, even though the difference is minimal.

8. Competitive Pricing

   Competitive pricing involves setting prices in line with or slightly below the prices of competitors. This strategy is common in industries with many similar products or services. For example, fast-food chains often adjust their prices based on what their competitors are offering to stay competitive in the market.

9. Price Skimming

   Price skimming entails setting a high initial price for a new product, capitalizing on early adopters willing to pay a premium. As time passes and demand from this segment wanes, the price is gradually reduced to attract more price-sensitive customers. Apple's strategy with the iPhone is a classic example of price skimming.

10. Geographic Pricing

    Geographic pricing involves adjusting prices based on the geographic location of customers. For instance, companies may charge different prices for the same product in different regions or countries due to variations in demand, cost structures, or local market conditions.

Real-World Insights: Uber's Surge Pricing

Uber, the ride-sharing giant, is a prime example of dynamic pricing in action. During periods of high demand or limited driver availability, Uber implements surge pricing. This means that the fare for a ride can increase significantly, sometimes reaching multiple times the normal rate. While this approach may initially seem counterintuitive, it's a powerful way to balance supply and demand, ensuring that customers can find rides even during peak times while incentivizing more drivers to come online.

The Art of Pricing Psychology

Pricing strategies are not just about setting numbers; they're about understanding human psychology and behaviour. Here are some fascinating insights into pricing psychology:

1. The Left-Digit Effect
   Consumers tend to focus on the leftmost digit when assessing prices. Thus, pricing a product at $9.99 instead of $10 can lead to significantly higher sales because it creates the perception of a lower cost.

2. Anchor Pricing
   Anchor pricing involves presenting a higher-priced option (the anchor) next to the product or service you want customers to choose. The higher price sets a reference point, making the target price seem more reasonable. For example, a high-end restaurant might list a deluxe steak at $100 on the menu to make a $50 steak seem like a bargain.

3. Price Bundling
   Bundling products together can influence consumer behaviour. Customers often perceive bundles as offering greater value, even if the total price is higher than buying individual items. This perception can lead to increased sales and higher overall revenue.

4. The Decoy Effect
   The decoy effect involves introducing a third, less-attractive option to manipulate consumer choices. For example, a coffee

shop might offer a small coffee for $2, a medium for $3, and a large for $4. The medium coffee serves as the decoy, making the large coffee seem like a better deal encouraging customers to spend more.

5. Loss Aversion

   Consumers tend to be more sensitive to potential losses than gains. This phenomenon is known as loss aversion. Pricing strategies that emphasize the potential cost savings, such as "Save $50" instead of "50% off," can be more compelling to customers.

Adapting Pricing Strategies to Your Business

The choice of pricing strategy depends on various factors, including your product or service, target market, competition, and market conditions. Moreover, pricing strategies are not static; they can evolve over time as your business grows and market dynamics change. Successful companies continually analyse pricing data, conduct market research, and monitor consumer behaviour to refine their pricing strategies.

Pricing strategies are a blend of art and science. By understanding the psychology of pricing and applying a range of strategic approaches, businesses can optimize their pricing models to maximize revenue, enhance customer satisfaction, and stay competitive in today's dynamic marketplaces. Whether you're setting a premium price to convey exclusivity or employing dynamic pricing to respond to changing demand, pricing strategies play a pivotal role in the world of sales negotiation.

The art of pricing lies not just in numbers but in the mastery of human perceptions and behaviour.

Defending Your Pricing

Pricing is a delicate balance. Set it too high, and you risk scaring away potential customers; set it too low, and you may compromise profitability. To master the art of pricing defense, sales professionals must be equipped with strategies that communicate value, answer objections, and ultimately convince customers that the price aligns with the benefits.

The Value Proposition

Defending your pricing starts with a strong value proposition. Customers need to understand what sets your product or service apart from the competition. It's not just about what they get; it's about what they gain.

Example: Apple's Premium Pricing

Apple's pricing strategy for its products is often higher than that of competitors. However, Apple successfully defends its premium pricing by emphasizing the exceptional build quality, user experience, and ecosystem integration that its products offer. Customers perceive the value in terms of reliability, aesthetics, and seamless connectivity.

Addressing Cost vs. Value

Customers naturally weigh the cost of a product or service against the value they expect to receive. As a sales professional, your task is to illustrate that the value far exceeds the cost.

Example: Amazon Prime

Amazon Prime, a subscription service, defends its annual fee by offering a multitude of benefits, such as free two-day shipping, access to streaming content, exclusive deals, and more. The perceived value of these benefits surpasses the subscription cost, making it an attractive proposition for customers.

Emphasizing ROI (Return on Investment)

For B2B sales, where purchases often involve significant investments, focusing on the ROI can be a powerful pricing defense strategy.

Example: Salesforce

Salesforce, a leading CRM platform, positions itself as a solution that can significantly boost a company's sales and customer relationships. They emphasize how the efficiency and insights gained from their platform justify the expense, showing a clear ROI for businesses.

Highlighting Unique Features

If your product or service offers unique features or capabilities, make sure customers are aware of them and understand their significance.

Example: Tesla

Tesla's electric vehicles are known for their advanced Autopilot features. Tesla defends its premium pricing by showcasing the safety and convenience benefits of Autopilot, highlighting how it sets Tesla apart from traditional car manufacturers.

The Role of Storytelling

Stories are powerful tools for defending pricing. They allow you to connect with customers on an emotional level and illustrate the real-world impact of your product or service.

Example: TOMS Shoes

TOMS Shoes not only sells footwear but also a compelling story. For every pair of shoes purchased, TOMS donates a pair to a child in need. This story adds depth to their pricing defense, emphasizing the value of making a difference with every purchase.

Handling Objections

Customers may raise objections about the price. It's essential to be prepared to address these objections effectively.

Example: Zendesk

Zendesk, a customer service software company, addresses pricing objections by offering a range of plans, including a lower-cost option for smaller businesses. They provide clear pricing information and have a support team ready to explain the value of each plan, helping customers find a suitable solution within their budget.

Providing Evidence

Data and evidence can strengthen your pricing defense. This can include case studies, customer testimonials, or industry benchmarks that demonstrate the value of your product or service.

Example: Slack

Slack, a messaging and collaboration platform, showcases case studies on its website that detail how businesses have achieved improved productivity and efficiency by using Slack. These case studies serve as evidence of the platform's value, helping justify its pricing.

The Power of Transparency

Being transparent about your pricing can build trust and strengthen your pricing defense.

Example: Buffer

Buffer, a social media management platform, is transparent about its pricing structure. They provide detailed information about what each plan includes and how pricing scales based on the number of social media accounts and team members. This transparency helps potential customers understand the cost and value.

Discounts and Incentives

Offering discounts or incentives can be an effective way to defend pricing, especially when customers are price-sensitive.

Example: Amazon Prime Student

Amazon offers a discounted Amazon Prime membership for students. By providing a reduced price and access to Prime benefits, they defend their pricing while appealing to a specific demographic.

The Art of Defending Pricing

Negotiation skills are vital when defending pricing, especially in B2B sales. The ability to find mutually beneficial solutions can lead to successful outcomes.

Example: HubSpot

HubSpot, a marketing and CRM platform, offers flexibility in pricing and contract terms. They work with customers to tailor solutions to their specific needs, demonstrating a willingness to negotiate and accommodate varying budgets.

Customization and Personalization

Allowing customers to customize or personalize their purchases can help them see the value in your pricing.

Example: Nike By You

Nike offers a customization service called "Nike By You," where customers can design their own sneakers. This level of personalization justifies higher pricing because customers are getting a unique product tailored to their preferences.

Monitoring and Feedback

Continuously monitor customer feedback and use it to refine your pricing strategy. Customer insights can help you adapt and defend your pricing effectively.

Example: Netflix

Netflix periodically adjusts its pricing based on customer feedback and market conditions. They learn from user preferences and behaviours to offer pricing tiers that cater to different viewing habits, defending their pricing in a highly competitive streaming market.

Defending your pricing is not just about convincing customers to pay a certain amount; it's about demonstrating the value, addressing objections, and finding mutually beneficial solutions. By mastering these pricing defence strategies and drawing inspiration from innovative examples, sales professionals can navigate pricing negotiations with confidence, ensuring that both buyers and sellers recognize the fair value in every transaction. In the ever-evolving landscape of sales negotiation, effective pricing defence is a skill that can lead to successful outcomes and long-term customer relationships.

Handling Price Objections

Price objections are common in sales negotiations, and they often stem from customers' natural desire to seek the best deal. However, savvy sales professionals can turn these objections into opportunities by employing innovative strategies that showcase the value, affordability, and overall benefits of their offerings.

Framing the Conversation

Price objections are often about perception. By framing the conversation in the right way, you can guide customers toward a more favourable view of your pricing.

Example: Starbucks

Starbucks uses the "tall, grande, venti" size options to frame the conversation about coffee. By offering a larger size, they make the medium option (grande) seem more reasonable, increasing the average transaction value.

The Power of Bundling

Bundling products or services can help mitigate price objections. When customers see the combined value of a package, they are less likely to focus solely on the individual prices.

Example: Microsoft Office 365

Microsoft bundles its Office applications, cloud storage, and other services into Office 365 subscriptions. This approach showcases the comprehensive value of the bundle compared to purchasing each component separately.

Overcoming the "Sticker Shock"

Customers often experience "sticker shock" when they see the total price upfront. Innovative pricing strategies can mitigate this shock and make the purchase more palatable.

Example: Peloton

Peloton, a fitness equipment company, offers financing options that break down the cost of their exercise bikes and subscriptions into monthly payments. This approach makes the purchase more manageable and lessens the impact of the initial price.

The Role of Customer Education

Innovation can also involve educating customers about the long-term value of your product or service, helping them see beyond the initial cost.

Example: Electric Vehicles (EVs)

Electric vehicle manufacturers educate potential buyers about the cost savings associated with EVs, such as lower fuel expenses and reduced maintenance. By highlighting these long-term benefits, they justify the higher upfront price of EVs.

Demonstrating ROI (Return on Investment)

For B2B sales, demonstrating a clear return on investment can be a game-changer when handling price objections.

Example: Salesforce

Salesforce uses case studies and data-driven insights to showcase how their CRM platform can lead to increased sales, improved customer relationships, and higher revenue for businesses. This approach helps justify the investment in their software.

The Art of Value Presentation

Innovative sales professionals know that it's not just about the price; it's about the value that comes with it. Presenting this value effectively can overcome price objections.

Example: Apple's iPhone

Apple focuses on the overall experience and benefits of owning an iPhone rather than just its technical specifications. Their marketing emphasizes the seamless integration of hardware and software, the App Store's vast ecosystem, and the device's durability, helping customers see the value beyond the iPhone's price tag.

Personalized Pricing Solutions

In some cases, innovative sales professionals can offer personalized pricing solutions that cater to individual customer needs.

Example: SaaS Companies

Many Software as a Service (SaaS) companies offer tiered pricing plans to accommodate different customer requirements. This flexibility allows customers to choose a plan that aligns with their budget and specific needs.

Leveraging Social Proof

Social proof, such as customer reviews, testimonials, and success stories, can be a powerful tool to address price objections.

Example: Amazon

Amazon's product pages feature customer reviews and ratings prominently. When potential buyers see positive feedback and experiences from others, they are more likely to perceive the product's value and be willing to pay the listed price.

The Role of Incentives

Innovative incentives can tip the scales in your favour when handling price objections.

Example: Airlines and Loyalty Programs

Airlines often offer frequent flyer programs that reward loyal customers with perks like free flights, upgrades, and lounge access. These incentives can make customers more willing to pay the ticket price, knowing they'll receive added value in the long run.

The Art of Negotiation

Negotiation is a skill where creativity and innovation can shine. Offering concessions or additional benefits can be a strategic way to handle price objections.

Example: Car Dealerships

Car dealerships often negotiate by offering complimentary services like extended warranties, maintenance packages, or lower financing rates to address price objections and sweeten the deal for customers.

Tailoring the Conversation

Innovative sales professionals tailor their conversations to address specific customer concerns and objections.

Example: Insurance Companies

Insurance agents assess individual customer needs and offer tailored policies. By addressing a customer's unique circumstances, they can justify the policy's price and coverage, making it more appealing.

Providing a Sense of Urgency

Creating a sense of urgency can encourage customers to act despite price objections.

Example: E-commerce Flash Sales

Many e-commerce platforms use flash sales with limited-time offers and countdowns to prompt customers to make quick decisions. The urgency created by these sales often trumps price objections.

Monitoring and Learning

Innovation in handling price objections doesn't stop at the initial sale. Continuously monitoring objections and learning from them can lead to improved strategies.

Example: Amazon Customer Feedback

Amazon encourages customers to provide feedback on product prices. By analysing this data, they can adjust pricing and promotions to better align with customer expectations.

Handling price objections requires innovative thinking, creative strategies, and a deep understanding of customer psychology. By framing conversations effectively, showcasing value, addressing concerns, and offering personalized solutions, sales professionals can turn price objections into opportunities for closing deals. Innovation in pricing defence is not just about reducing prices but about demonstrating the value that customers receive in exchange for their investment. In the dynamic world of sales negotiation, mastering the art of handling price objections is a skill that can lead to successful outcomes and long-term customer loyalty.

Negotiating Discounts & Terms

Discount negotiation involves striking a balance between offering attractive pricing to customers and maintaining profitability for your business. Innovative discount negotiation techniques can help achieve this equilibrium.

Value-Added Discounts

Instead of straightforward price reductions, consider offering value-added discounts that provide additional benefits to customers.

Example: Amazon Prime

Amazon Prime offers a value-added discount by bundling benefits like free two-day shipping, streaming services, and exclusive deals into a subscription. While customers pay an annual fee, they perceive significant value beyond just shipping discounts.

Quantity-Based Discounts

Encourage larger purchases by offering quantity-based discounts that reward customers for buying in bulk.

Example: Wholesale Clubs

Wholesale clubs like Costco offer discounts on items when purchased in larger quantities. This approach incentivizes customers to buy more while benefiting from lower unit prices.

Loyalty Discounts

Reward loyal customers with discounts, fostering long-term relationships and repeat business.

Example: Starbucks Rewards

Starbucks offers loyalty program members discounts, free drinks, and personalized offers based on their purchasing history. This encourages customers to choose Starbucks for their coffee needs, even when other options are available.

Time-Limited Promotions

Create a sense of urgency with time-limited discounts, compelling customers to make a purchase decision quickly.

Example: Black Friday Sales

Retailers offer significant discounts on Black Friday, creating a frenzy of shoppers looking to take advantage of limited-time deals. The urgency of the event encourages customers to buy now rather than later.

Tiered Pricing

Implement tiered pricing structures where discounts increase with larger purchases.

Example: SaaS Subscription Plans

Many Software as a Service (SaaS) providers offer tiered subscription plans. Customers receive more features and greater discounts as they upgrade to higher tiers, making it an attractive proposition for businesses of varying sizes.

Package Deals

Combine multiple products or services into package deals with bundled discounts.

Example: Cable and Internet Bundles

Cable and internet providers often bundle their services with discounts for customers who subscribe to both. This approach encourages customers to get more value from a single provider.

Innovative Terms Negotiation

Negotiating favourable terms can be equally important as discounts. Innovative terms negotiation involves finding mutually beneficial solutions that address customers' needs while safeguarding your business interests.

1. Flexible Payment Options

Offer flexible payment terms to accommodate customers' cash flow and budget constraints.

Example: Car Dealerships

Car dealerships often provide financing options with flexible payment terms. Customers can choose from various loan durations and down payment options to suit their financial situation.

2. Extended Warranty and Support

Enhance the value of your product or service by including extended warranties or support packages.

Example: Electronics Retailers

Electronics retailers offer extended warranties that cover repairs and replacements beyond the manufacturer's warranty. This additional assurance can justify a higher upfront purchase price for customers.

3. Satisfaction Guarantees

Provide satisfaction guarantees or return policies that reduce the perceived risk of the purchase.

Example: Zappos

Zappos, an online shoe retailer, offers a 365-day return policy with free shipping both ways. This guarantee instills confidence in customers, making them more likely to purchase shoes online.

4. Customization Options

Allow customers to customize products or services to meet their needs better.

Example: Dell Computers

Dell allows customers to customize the specifications of their computers, from processors to graphics cards. This customization option ensures that customers get exactly what they want, even if it means paying a premium.

5. Early Payment Discounts

Incentivize early payments with discounts to improve your cash flow.

Example: Utility Companies

Utility companies often offer discounts to customers who pay their bills early or set up automatic payments. This encourages timely payments and reduces the administrative burden of chasing overdue accounts.

6. Subscription Models

Introduce subscription-based models that provide ongoing value to customers while ensuring recurring revenue for your business.

Example: Streaming Services

Streaming services like Netflix and Spotify offer monthly subscriptions that grant access to a vast library of content. Customers benefit from a continuous stream of entertainment, while the businesses maintain a steady income stream.

7. Vendor Financing

Explore vendor financing options to help customers afford larger purchases.

Example: Car Manufacturers

Car manufacturers often provide financing options through their own financing arms or partnerships with banks. This makes it easier for customers to afford vehicles and can lead to more sales.

Example: Business Software Licensing

Business software providers often negotiate customized licensing agreements with enterprises. These agreements can include volume discounts, flexible terms, and additional support services. By tailoring agreements to meet specific business needs, software providers secure long-term partnerships and revenue streams.

Negotiating discounts and terms is a dynamic and strategic process that involves finding innovative solutions that benefit both customers and businesses. By offering value-added discounts, flexible payment options, and mutually beneficial terms, sales professionals can create win-win situations that lead to successful outcomes and long-term customer relationships. In the ever-evolving landscape of sales negotiation, mastering the art of negotiating discounts and terms is a skill that can drive growth, customer satisfaction, and profitability.

CHAPTER 8

CLOSING THE DEAL

*I*n the world of sales, the art of "closing the deal" stands as the culmination of intricate negotiations, compelling presentations, and unwavering perseverance. This pivotal moment marks the juncture where prospects transform into loyal customers and transactions solidify into successful partnerships. In this chapter, we will explore the strategies, tactics, and psychological insights that empower sales professionals to seal the deal with finesse, ensuring that both parties walk away satisfied and eager to embark on a mutually beneficial journey. Closing the deal is not merely the end; it is the beginning of lasting relationships and the gateway to sustained success in the realm of sales.

Recognizing Buying Signals

Sales professionals often compare their role to that of detectives, keenly observing and interpreting various clues to gauge a potential customer's level of interest and readiness to buy. Recognizing buying signals is not just about identifying when to close a deal; it's about understanding when to offer guidance, address concerns, and tailor your approach to the prospect's needs.

Verbal Cues

Verbal cues are the spoken hints and expressions that reveal a potential customer's intentions and level of interest.

Example: Explicit Buying Statements

When a customer says, "I'm ready to make a decision," or "I think this is exactly what I need," these explicit statements are strong buying signals indicating a readiness to move forward.

Example: Questions About Specifics

When a prospect starts asking detailed questions about product specifications, pricing, or delivery, it demonstrates a desire to dig deeper and gather information crucial for making a decision.

Non-Verbal Cues

Non-verbal cules encompass body language, facial expressions, and gestures that provide valuable insights into a prospect's emotional state and level of engagement.

Example: Leaning In

If a potential customer leans forward during a presentation or discussion, it indicates increased interest and engagement. This subtle movement signifies that they are leaning toward a positive decision.

Example: Facial Expressions

A prospect's facial expressions can reveal a lot. A smile, nodding in agreement, or an attentive gaze can all signal receptivity and interest. On the other hand, furrowed brows or crossed arms may indicate skepticism or uncertainty.

Behavioural Cues

Behavioral cues refer to actions or behaviours that suggest a potential customer's readiness to take the next step.

Example: Requesting a Quote or Proposal

When a prospect actively requests a formal quote, proposal, or contract, it's a strong indication that they are seriously considering your offering and are moving closer to a purchasing decision.

Example: Engaging in Follow-Up Conversations

If a prospect initiates follow-up discussions about specific terms, features, or customization options, it signals a deeper level of engagement and a willingness to explore the details of the deal.

Financial Cues

Financial cues involve indications that the prospect is evaluating the financial aspects of the purchase.

Example: Inquiring About Pricing Options

When a potential customer starts asking about pricing plans, discounts, or payment terms, it suggests that they are not only interested but also considering the financial feasibility of the purchase.

Example: Expressing Budget Flexibility

If a prospect mentions flexibility in their budget or willingness to allocate resources, it implies they are open to investment discussions and are evaluating the value of your offering.

Time-Related Cues

Time-related cues pertain to indications that the prospect has a timeline or urgency associated with their decision-making process.

Example: Mentioning Deadlines

When a potential customer brings up deadlines or time-sensitive needs, it signals that they are actively considering a solution within a specific timeframe.

Example: Expressing a Desire to Move Quickly

If a prospect emphasizes the importance of a swift implementation or expresses a desire to get started promptly, it indicates a sense of urgency and readiness to make a purchase.

Engagement on Multiple Touchpoints

Prospects who engage with your company across various touchpoints, such as attending webinars, downloading resources, and participating in demonstrations, are sending a strong buying signal. This multichannel engagement demonstrates a significant level of interest and investment in the decision-making process.

Example: Engaging in Webinars and Demos

A prospect who attends your webinar signs up for a product demonstration, and downloads relevant whitepapers is actively seeking information and engaging deeply with your offerings.

Innovative Techniques for Recognizing Buying Signals

In addition to traditional cues, there are innovative techniques that sales professionals can employ to enhance their ability to recognize buying signals effectively:

1. Social Listening

Monitor social media platforms and online forums for discussions related to your industry, products, or services. Prospects often share their opinions and needs online, providing valuable insights into their interests and potential buying signals.

Example: Twitter Hashtags

By tracking relevant hashtags on Twitter, a sales professional can identify users discussing topics related to their offerings. Engaging with these users can lead to valuable conversations and the recognition of buying signals.

2. Data Analytics

Leverage data analytics tools to track prospect behaviour on your website, such as page visits, content downloads, and time spent on specific pages. Analysing this data can help identify which prospects are actively researching and engaging with your offerings.

Example: Website Heatmaps

Heatmaps can show which areas of your website attract the most attention. If prospects are spending a significant amount of time on product pages or pricing information, it indicates a high level of interest.

3. AI-Powered Chatbots

Implement AI-powered chatbots on your website to engage with visitors in real time. Chatbots can collect information about visitor intent and interests, helping identify potential buying signals.

Example: Chatbot Conversations

A chatbot can initiate conversations with visitors, asking questions like, "What specific features are you looking for?" or "Are you considering a purchase in the near future?" Based on responses, the chatbot can recognize buying signals and escalate the conversation to a human sales representative.

Real-Life Success Stories

Let's explore real-life success stories that illustrate the importance of recognizing buying signals:

Example: HubSpot's Inbound Marketing

HubSpot, a leading inbound marketing and sales software company, emphasizes the importance of recognizing buying signals through inbound marketing tactics. By analysing website visitor behaviour, engagement with content, and lead scoring, HubSpot identifies prospects who are actively exploring its solutions. This recognition of buying signals enables the sales team to reach out at the right time with tailored messages and offers, resulting in higher conversion rates.

Example: Amazon's Algorithmic Insights

Amazon employs advanced algorithms to analyse customer behaviour on its platform. By recognizing buying signals such as browsing history, product searches, and items added to the shopping cart, Amazon provides personalized product recommendations and timely promotions. This data-driven approach enhances the likelihood of customers making a purchase.

Recognizing buying signals is an art that requires keen observation, active listening, and a deep understanding of prospect behaviour. By paying attention to verbal and non-verbal cues, assessing behavioral patterns, and leveraging innovative techniques, sales professionals can identify the right moments to guide prospects toward a purchase. This skill not only leads to more successful deal closures but also fosters trust, as prospects appreciate a sales approach that aligns with their needs and readiness to buy. In the dynamic world of sales, the ability to recognize buying signals is a valuable asset that can drive sales growth and long-lasting customer relationships.

The Art of Closing Techniques

Closing a deal is the culmination of a sales journey, and it requires finesse, adaptability, and persuasive skills. Sales professionals utilize various closing techniques to guide potential customers toward a positive decision. Let's delve into innovative approaches that go beyond the traditional methods.

The Assumptive Close

The assumptive close is an assertive technique where the salesperson assumes the prospect is ready to make a purchase. By phrasing questions and statements in a way that implies the sale is already a given, it encourages the prospect to agree and move forward.

Example: Restaurant Reservation

Imagine a scenario where a restaurant host says, "Would you prefer a table by the window or in the center of the dining area?" This question assumes that the customers have already decided to dine at the restaurant, and their choice of seating is the only decision left to make.

The Choice Close

The choice close provides prospects with options, allowing them to select from two or more alternatives. This technique empowers prospects by giving them a sense of control over their decision.

Example: Clothing Store

In a clothing store, a salesperson might say, "Would you like the red dress or the blue one?" This approach presents options and encourages the prospect to choose, making them feel more involved in the decision-making process.

The Negative Close

The negative close is a method where the salesperson highlights the potential negative consequences of not making a purchase. Emphasizing what the prospect might miss out on or the problems they could face without the product or service motivates them to avoid those negative outcomes.

Example: Home Security System

A salesperson for a home security system might say, "Without a security system, your home could be vulnerable to break-ins and theft. Don't wait until it's too late to protect your family and valuables."

The Puppy-Dog Close

The puppy-dog close involves allowing the prospect to experience the product or service temporarily. This creates a sense of attachment, making it more challenging for the prospect to give it up.

Example: Car Test Drive

Car dealerships often use the puppy-dog close by encouraging potential buyers to take a test drive. Once the prospect experiences the comfort, performance, and features of the car, they are less likely to walk away from the opportunity to own it.

The Summary Close

The summary close is a technique where the salesperson summarizes the key benefits and advantages of the product or service, emphasizing how it addresses the prospect's needs and desires. This recap reinforces the value proposition before asking for the commitment.

Example: SaaS Sales

In a 'software as a service' (SaaS) sales pitch, the salesperson might say, "Just to recap, our platform streamlines your workflow, increases efficiency, and reduces costs. It's a powerful tool to help your team achieve their goals. Shall we move forward with the subscription?"

The Question Close

The question close involves asking a closing question directly to the prospect. This straightforward approach puts the decision in the prospect's hands.

Example: Real Estate

A real estate agent might ask, "So, do you see yourself living in this house and making it your home?" This question prompts the prospect to provide a definitive answer regarding their interest in the property.

The Fear-of-Missing-Out (FOMO) Close

The FOMO close leverages the prospect's fear of missing out on a valuable opportunity. It emphasizes the urgency and exclusivity of the offer, encouraging the prospect to act quickly.

Example: Limited-Time Discount

A salesperson promoting a limited-time discount might say, "This special offer is only available for the next 48 hours. Many customers have already taken advantage of it. If you delay, you might miss out on these savings."

Innovative Techniques for Closing Deals

In addition to traditional closing techniques, sales professionals can employ innovative approaches to seal the deal effectively:

1. Customized Trial Periods

Offering a customized trial period allows prospects to use the product or service with minimal commitment. This approach demonstrates confidence in the offering's value and encourages prospects to experience it first-hand.

Example: Software Trials

Software companies often offer free trial periods with customizable features. Prospects can use the software according to their needs, gaining a deep understanding of its capabilities.

2. The Value Stack Close

The value stack close involves creating a visual representation of the value a prospect will receive from the purchase. This can be in the form of a chart or list that highlights the benefits and features, making the value tangible and compelling.

Example: Investment Advisors

Investment advisors often use the value stack close by presenting a visual breakdown of potential returns, tax benefits, and long-term growth opportunities associated with an investment.

3. The Collaborative Close

The collaborative close involves working closely with the prospect to create a personalized solution. Involving the prospect in the decision-making process and tailoring the offer to their needs fosters a sense of partnership and commitment.

Example: Consulting Services

Consulting firms collaborate with clients to define project scopes, deliverables, and timelines. This collaborative approach ensures that the client's specific needs are met.

Real-Life Success Stories

Let's explore real-life success stories that illustrate the effectiveness of innovative closing techniques:

Example: Apple's Product Launch Events

Apple's product launch events are a masterclass in the art of closing deals through anticipation and excitement. By unveiling new products with compelling features and limited availability, Apple creates a sense of urgency and exclusivity that drives customers to make purchases immediately.

Example: Amazon's One-Click Ordering

Amazon introduced the one-click ordering feature, allowing customers to make a purchase with a single click. This streamlined and frictionless process eliminates barriers to making impulse purchases, leading to increased sales and customer satisfaction.

Example: Airbnb's Booking Process

Airbnb's booking process is designed to encourage travellers to commit to a reservation. Features like instant booking and transparent pricing give users confidence and convenience, making it easy for them to close the deal and secure accommodations.

Mastering the art of closing techniques is essential for sales professionals aiming to convert prospects into satisfied customers. By employing innovative approaches that go beyond traditional methods, such as customized trial periods, value stack presentations, and collaborative closes, sales professionals can navigate the complexities of modern sales with finesse. The ability to close deals effectively is not just about persuasion; it's about creating meaningful connections, addressing needs, and providing value. In the ever-evolving landscape of sales, closing techniques are the key to turning prospects into loyal customers and driving business success.

Overcoming Final Hurdles

In the world of sales, the final stages of negotiation often present unique challenges that require creativity, persistence, and strategic thinking. These hurdles can take various forms, from pricing objections to contract concerns, and they can significantly impact the decision-making process of potential customers. To address these challenges effectively, sales professionals employ innovative strategies.

 # Innovative Pricing Solutions

Pricing objections are among the most common final hurdles in sales. Prospects may have concerns about costs, budget constraints, or the perceived value of the offering. Innovative pricing solutions can help alleviate these concerns and facilitate the path to closing the deal.

Example: The Freemium Model

Many software companies offer freemium models, providing a basic version of their product for free while offering premium features at a cost. This approach allows prospects to experience the product's value before committing to a paid plan, addressing pricing concerns and encouraging upgrades.

Example: Flexible Payment Structures

Some businesses offer flexible payment structures that cater to their customers' financial situations. This might include monthly payments, installment plans, or deferred payment options. By accommodating different budgets, sales professionals can overcome pricing objections.

Persuasive Storytelling

Storytelling is a powerful tool that can help sales professionals overcome final hurdles. Sharing success stories, customer testimonials, and case studies can illustrate the positive impact of the product or service and address concerns effectively.

Example: Customer Testimonials

A B2B software salesperson may share a testimonial from a similar company that saw a significant increase in productivity and revenue after implementing their solution. Hearing about real-world success can alleviate doubts and inspire confidence.

Example: Case Studies

A sales professional selling marketing services might present a case study showcasing how their strategies helped a client achieve a substantial ROI. This evidence-based approach demonstrates the potential value of the offering.

Negotiation Transparency

Transparency in negotiations can build trust and reduce skepticism during the final stages of a deal. Sales professionals who openly discuss terms, pricing, and contract details can foster a sense of partnership and collaboration with the prospect.

Example: Mutual Concession Sharing

During negotiations, both parties can openly share their concessions. For instance, a salesperson may say, "In the spirit of fairness, we're willing to offer a discount if you commit to a longer-term contract. What concessions can you make to move forward?" This approach encourages reciprocity and a win-win mentality.

Example: Transparent Contract Reviews

When discussing contract terms, sales professionals can provide a clear explanation of each clause and its implications. They may even offer to highlight and discuss potential areas of concern upfront. This level of transparency can alleviate worries about hidden terms and conditions.

Creating a Sense of Urgency

Creating a sense of urgency is a time-tested strategy to overcome final hurdles. By emphasizing limited-time offers, exclusive bonuses, or impending changes, sales professionals can motivate prospects to make decisions more promptly.

Example: Limited-Time Discounts

Many retailers employ limited-time discounts and promotions to encourage immediate purchases. Phrases like "this offer expires in 24 hours" can prompt prospects to take action.

Example: Product Availability Alerts

E-commerce platforms often use notifications like "Only two items left in stock" to create urgency. This encourages buyers to act swiftly to secure the product.

Anticipating and Addressing Concerns

Sales professionals can overcome final hurdles by proactively identifying and addressing potential concerns or objections that might arise. By pre-emptively providing solutions and explanations, they can build confidence and alleviate doubts.

Example: Comprehensive FAQs and Resources

Sales teams can create comprehensive FAQs and resources that address common questions and concerns. Prospects can access these materials to find answers and gain clarity.

Example: Dedicated Account Managers

Assigning dedicated account managers to customers can be a proactive way to address concerns. These managers can serve as a single point of contact for ongoing support and assistance, ensuring that any issues are resolved promptly.

Real-Life Success Stories

Let's explore real-life success stories that illustrate how innovative strategies have helped overcome final hurdles in sales:

Example: Apple's iPhone Launch

Apple's iPhone launch strategy incorporates elements of pricing innovation and creating a sense of urgency. Apple often releases new iPhone models with premium pricing, but they also offer trade-in programs that reduce the cost for customers. Additionally, they create anticipation by announcing limited quantities and release dates, which encourages early adoption.

Example: Amazon Prime's Value Proposition

Amazon Prime successfully addresses pricing concerns through a unique value proposition. While the annual subscription fee may seem steep to some, it includes a wide range of benefits, such as free shipping, streaming services, and exclusive deals. Amazon Prime members perceive significant value beyond just the pricing, making it an attractive offering.

Overcoming final hurdles in sales negotiations is a testament to the adaptability and creativity of sales professionals. By employing innovative pricing solutions, persuasive storytelling, negotiation transparency, creating a sense of urgency, and proactively addressing concerns, sales professionals can navigate the last obstacles and secure successful deals. These strategies not only lead to successful transactions but also foster trust, build long-term relationships, and turn prospects into loyal customers. In the ever-evolving landscape of sales, the ability to overcome final hurdles is a valuable asset that drives growth and business success.

Ensuring Smooth Transitions to Implementation

A smooth transition from the sales process to implementation is essential for both the customer and the selling organization.

It sets the stage for a successful partnership, reinforces the value proposition, and minimizes potential disruptions. However, this transition can be fraught with challenges that require innovative solutions.

Alignment and Expectation Management

Ensuring that the customer's expectations align with the product or service's capabilities is paramount. Misaligned expectations can lead to dissatisfaction and strained relationships.

Example: SaaS Onboarding

A Software as a Service (SaaS) provider conducts comprehensive onboarding sessions with new customers. During these sessions, they proactively discuss the product's features, limitations, and customization options. This transparency helps manage customer expectations and align them with the software's capabilities.

Effective Communication Channels

Smooth transitions necessitate effective communication channels between the sales team and the implementation or customer success team. This ensures that crucial information and insights gathered during the sales process are seamlessly transferred.

Example: Salesforce's Account Handoffs

Salesforce, a leading CRM provider, employs a structured account handoff process. Once a sale is closed, the sales team collaborates with the implementation team to transfer all relevant customer information, including specific needs, goals, and preferences. This facilitates a seamless transition and provides a solid foundation for implementation.

Customized Implementation Plans

Each customer is unique, and their requirements may vary. Creating customized implementation plans tailored to the customer's specific needs is essential for a successful transition.

Example: Enterprise Software Implementation

In the enterprise software space, providers often offer different implementation plans based on the customer's size, industry, and complexity. These tailored plans include customized training, data migration strategies, and ongoing support to address the unique challenges of each customer.

Ongoing Support and Training

Post-implementation support and training are critical for ensuring that customers derive maximum value from the product or service.

Example: LinkedIn Learning

LinkedIn Learning, a platform for online courses, offers post-implementation support through a range of resources. Customers have access to a library of training materials, webinars, and a responsive customer support team. This ongoing support helps users continuously enhance their skills.

Innovative Strategies for Smooth Transitions

In addition to traditional approaches, sales professionals can employ innovative strategies to ensure smooth transitions:

1. AI-Powered Transition Assistants

Leveraging artificial intelligence (AI) for transition assistance can streamline the process. AI can analyze customer data and provide personalized recommendations for a smoother implementation.

Example: Chatbots for Transition Assistance

Implementing chatbots with AI capabilities allows customers to ask questions and receive tailored guidance during the transition. These chatbots can also collect feedback, ensuring continuous improvement in the transition process.

2. Gamification of Onboarding

Gamification techniques can make onboarding and transition processes engaging and interactive. This approach helps customers quickly grasp product features and functionality.

Example: Duolingo's Gamified Language Learning

Duolingo gamifies the language-learning process by awarding points and virtual rewards for completing lessons. This approach keeps users engaged and motivated throughout their language-learning journey.

3. Predictive Analytics for Proactive Support

Predictive analytics can be used to identify potential challenges or roadblocks that customers might face during implementation. Sales professionals can then proactively address these issues.

Example: Predictive Maintenance in Manufacturing

In the manufacturing industry, predictive analytics are used to forecast equipment maintenance needs. This proactive approach prevents costly downtime and ensures a smooth transition to new equipment.

4. Self-Service Implementation Portals

Providing customers with self-service implementation portals empowers them to take control of the transition process. These portals can offer step-by-step guides, resources, and troubleshooting assistance.

Example: Cloud Service Providers

Cloud service providers often offer self-service implementation portals where customers can configure and deploy services on their own. These portals include tutorials, documentation, and tools for a seamless setup process.

Real-Life Success Stories

Let's explore real-life success stories that highlight the importance of ensuring a smooth transition to implementation:

Example: Slack's Onboarding Experience

Slack, a popular team communication platform, offers a user-friendly onboarding process that seamlessly guides new customers through the platform's features. They provide interactive tutorials, tips, and prompts to help teams transition from email communication to Slack effectively.

Example: Tesla's Vehicle Deliveries

Tesla, the electric car manufacturer, goes beyond the sales process to ensure a smooth transition to vehicle ownership. They provide extensive resources, including instructional videos and a mobile app, to help customers understand their new electric vehicles and the charging infrastructure. This approach minimizes any challenges customers may face during the transition to electric mobility.

Ensuring a smooth transition to implementation is a critical aspect of sales that requires innovative strategies and meticulous planning. By aligning expectations, establishing effective communication channels, creating customized implementation plans, and providing ongoing support and training, sales professionals can facilitate successful transitions for their customers. Incorporating innovative approaches such as AI-powered transition assistants, gamification, predictive analytics, and self-service implementation portals can further enhance the process. In the dynamic world of sales, a seamless transition sets the stage for long-term customer satisfaction, loyalty, and success.

CHAPTER 9

NEGOTIATING IN COMPLEX SALES

*N*avigating the intricate landscape of complex sales domain demands a deep understanding of the multifaceted challenges and opportunities that arise in high-stakes business transactions. In this chapter, we delve into the art of negotiating within complex sales scenarios, where multiple stakeholders, intricate requirements, and substantial investments converge. By exploring innovative strategies and real-life examples, we uncover how adept sales professionals thrive in these intricate negotiations, forging partnerships and achieving mutually beneficial outcomes in even the most intricate of deals.

Dealing with Multiple Stakeholders

Complex sales negotiations often involve a multitude of stakeholders, each wielding varying degrees of influence and possessing distinct objectives. Effectively managing these stakeholders is pivotal to securing a successful deal. Let's delve into innovative approaches for dealing with multiple stakeholders:

Stakeholder Mapping

Before diving into negotiations, sales professionals can create a stakeholder map, identifying key individuals and their roles, interests, and power within the organization. This comprehensive understanding forms the foundation for strategic engagement.

Example: B2B Software Sales

In the sale of complex software solutions to enterprises, sales teams often create stakeholder maps that include C-suite executives, department heads, IT managers, and end-users. Each stakeholder's concerns, such as cost savings, efficiency improvements, or user-friendliness, are meticulously documented to inform the negotiation strategy.

Tailored Messaging

Crafting tailored messages that resonate with each stakeholder's interests and concerns is essential. Sales professionals can customize their value propositions to address the unique needs of various stakeholders.

Example: Pharmaceutical Sales

Pharmaceutical companies must navigate complex negotiations with healthcare providers, insurers, regulatory agencies, and patient advocacy groups. Tailored messaging ensures that each stakeholder perceives the benefits of a new medication differently.

Insurers may focus on cost-effectiveness, while patient advocacy groups prioritize safety and efficacy.

Facilitated Workshops

Facilitated workshops bring together multiple stakeholders to collaboratively define objectives, address concerns, and align on priorities. These sessions foster transparency, build consensus, and expedite decision-making.

Example: Construction Project Bidding

In the construction industry, contractors often conduct facilitated workshops with architects, project managers, subcontractors, and clients. These workshops help establish project goals, budgets, and timelines, ensuring that all stakeholders are aligned before negotiations proceed.

Influencer Engagement

Identifying and engaging key influencers within the stakeholder group can significantly impact the negotiation process. Building relationships with individuals who hold sway over others can help sway opinions and secure buy-in.

Example: Enterprise Software Implementation

In the sale of enterprise software, sales professionals may identify a vocal advocate within the client's organization—a respected manager or department head. By addressing this influencer's needs and concerns, they can garner support from other stakeholders who value the influencer's opinion.

Real-Life Success Stories

Let's explore real-life success stories that demonstrate the importance of dealing with multiple stakeholders effectively:

Example: Boeing's Aircraft Sales

Boeing, a global aerospace company, excels in navigating complex sales negotiations with airlines worldwide. These negotiations involve a myriad of stakeholders, including airline executives, pilots, engineers, maintenance teams, and finance departments. Boeing's sales teams customize their messaging for each group, emphasizing safety and performance to pilots, fuel efficiency to finance teams, and reliability to maintenance personnel. By addressing the unique interests of each stakeholder, Boeing secures multi-billion-dollar aircraft deals.

Example: Pharmaceutical Drug Approval

The pharmaceutical industry is known for its intricate negotiations with regulatory agencies, healthcare providers, insurers, and patient advocacy groups. In the case of a breakthrough drug for a rare disease, the pharmaceutical company developed tailored messaging for each stakeholder. They highlighted the drug's potential to save lives and reduce long-term healthcare costs for insurers while assuring regulators of its safety and efficacy. This comprehensive approach helped expedite drug approval and access for patients.

Dealing with multiple stakeholders in complex sales negotiations is an art that requires innovative strategies and a deep understanding of each stakeholder's interests and motivations. Stakeholder mapping, tailored messaging, facilitated workshops, and influencer engagement are invaluable tools for navigating this intricate landscape. Successful outcomes hinge on sales professionals' ability to create alignment, build consensus, and secure buy-in from diverse stakeholder groups. In the dynamic world of complex sales, the adept management of multiple stakeholders is the key to forging partnerships and achieving mutually beneficial results that propel business success.

Navigating B2B Sales Negotiations

B2B sales negotiations represent a multifaceted ecosystem where companies engage in high-value transactions, forging partnerships that impact industries and economies. To navigate this complex terrain effectively, sales professionals must deploy innovative strategies:

Solution-Centric Approach

In today's B2B landscape, sales professionals are shifting from product-centric to solution-centric approaches. They focus on understanding the unique challenges and objectives of each client, tailoring offerings that solve specific pain points and deliver tangible value.

Example: IBM's Watson for Oncology

IBM's Watson for Oncology is a prime example of a solution-centric approach in B2B sales. Rather than selling a product, IBM offers a cognitive computing system that assists oncologists in treatment decision-making. The solution is customized to each healthcare provider's needs, addressing the complexities of cancer treatment.

Co-Creation and Co-Innovation

Co-creation and co-innovation are collaborative strategies that involve clients in the development of products or services. By involving clients in the creative process, companies not only meet their unique needs but also strengthen client relationships.

Example: Procter & Gamble's Connect + Develop

Procter & Gamble launched the Connect + Develop program, inviting external partners, including suppliers, to collaborate on product innovation. This open innovation approach led to the creation of products such as the Swiffer cleaning system, which addressed a specific market need.

Data-Driven Decision-Making

In the digital age, data-driven decision-making is pivotal in B2B sales. Sales professionals leverage data analytics to gain insights into customer behaviour, preferences, and pain points, allowing for more informed negotiations.

Example: Salesforce's AI-Driven Sales Insights

Salesforce employs artificial intelligence to provide sales teams with predictive insights. By analysing customer data, Salesforce's AI tools help sales professionals identify which leads are more likely to convert, enabling them to prioritize negotiations effectively.

Value-Based Pricing

Value-based pricing has gained prominence in B2B sales. Companies determine prices based on the perceived value their offerings deliver to clients rather than the cost of production. This approach aligns pricing with the value clients receive.

Example: SaaS Subscription Pricing

Many 'software as a service' (SaaS) providers offer tiered subscription pricing based on features and usage. Clients pay more for advanced features or higher usage levels, reflecting the additional value these features provide.

Real-Life Success Stories

Let's delve into real-life success stories that illustrate the innovation and expertise required to navigate B2B sales negotiations effectively:

Example: GE Healthcare's Hospital Partnerships

GE Healthcare collaborates with hospitals and healthcare systems to provide innovative medical solutions. Rather than selling individual products, GE works with healthcare providers to co-create comprehensive solutions. For example, GE partners with hospitals to design efficient radiology departments, integrating imaging technology, workflow optimization, and training programs.

Navigating B2B sales negotiations requires an innovative and client-centric approach. Sales professionals must embrace solution-centric strategies, co-creation, data-driven insights, and value-based pricing to excel in this complex arena. The success stories of companies like IBM, Procter & Gamble, Salesforce, Boeing, and GE Healthcare demonstrate the impact of innovative approaches in shaping B2B deals that drive progress and propel industries forward. In the ever-evolving landscape of B2B sales, the art of negotiation is a catalyst for innovation, forging partnerships, and achieving remarkable outcomes that transcend traditional boundaries.

Handling Competitive Bidding Scenarios

Competitive bidding scenarios are common in various industries, from construction and technology to government contracts and service providers. They entail multiple entities vying for the same contract, project, or opportunity, often under stringent constraints. To excel in these scenarios, businesses and sales professionals must deploy innovative strategies:

 # Value Proposition Differentiation

In a mid of large number of competitors, standing out is essential. Sales professionals must craft unique value propositions that highlight what sets their offerings apart. This requires a deep understanding of the client's needs and priorities.

Example: SpaceX's Commercial Space Launches

SpaceX, led by Elon Musk, has disrupted the space launch industry by offering cost-effective, reusable rockets. Their value proposition revolves around drastically reducing launch costs and making space more accessible to commercial entities. This differentiation secured contracts with clients like NASA and satellite operators.

Collaborative Partnerships

In some competitive bidding scenarios, forming strategic partnerships can be a game-changer. Collaborating with complementary businesses can enhance the overall proposal and increase the chances of success.

Example: Joint Ventures in Construction

In the construction industry, joint ventures between construction companies with complementary specialties are common. One firm may excel in structural engineering, while another specializes in architectural design. By joining forces, they can present a comprehensive solution that appeals to clients seeking integrated services.

Innovative Pricing Models

Innovative pricing models can be a competitive advantage. Businesses can explore options such as performance-based pricing, subscription models, or value-based pricing to align their offerings with the client's objectives.

Example: Software as a service (SaaS) Subscription Pricing

Many SaaS providers offer subscription-based pricing with flexible tiers based on usage or features. Clients appreciate the transparency and scalability of such pricing models, as they can align costs with their needs.

Demonstration of Expertise

Demonstrating expertise through thought leadership, case studies, and a track record of successful projects can instill confidence in clients. It showcases a deep understanding of the industry and the ability to deliver results.

Example: McKinsey & Company's Thought Leadership

McKinsey & Company, a management consulting firm, regularly publishes thought leadership articles and reports on industry trends and challenges. This positions them as experts and trusted advisors in their field, attracting clients seeking strategic guidance.

Real-Life Success Stories

Let's delve into real-life success stories that highlight the innovation and expertise required to excel in competitive bidding scenarios:

Example: Defence Contracting Competitions

In the Defence industry, competitive bidding scenarios are common for contracts involving complex systems, such as fighter jets or submarines. Companies like Lockheed Martin, Boeing, and Northrop Grumman regularly compete for lucrative defence contracts. Their proposals encompass not only technical specifications but also economic impact, job creation, and long-term sustainment plans. Winning these contracts requires a combination of technical prowess, financial strength, and innovative solutions.

Handling competitive bidding scenarios is a multifaceted challenge that demands innovative thinking, strategic differentiation, and a deep understanding of client needs. In a world where businesses constantly vie for opportunities, the ability to stand out through unique value propositions, collaborative partnerships, innovative pricing models, and a demonstration of expertise is paramount. In the ever-competitive landscape of bidding scenarios, innovation is the key to emerging victorious and achieving remarkable outcomes that drive business growth and success.

Managing Long Sales Cycles

Long sales cycles are a characteristic of many industries, including B2B, enterprise software, real estate, and healthcare. These extended journeys involve multiple decision-makers, intricate requirements, and often substantial investments. To excel in managing long sales cycles, businesses and sales professionals must deploy innovative strategies:

Relationship-Centric Approach

Long sales cycles often necessitate a focus on building strong, enduring relationships with clients. Sales professionals should nurture connections, providing value and support throughout the extended process.

Example: Salesforce's Account Management

Salesforce, a leading CRM provider, places a strong emphasis on relationship management. Their account executives maintain continuous engagement with clients, understanding their evolving needs and goals. This approach not only sustains long-term relationships but also positions Salesforce as a trusted partner.

Customized Content and Education

During extended sales cycles, clients seek in-depth knowledge and customized solutions. Sales professionals must deliver educational content that addresses client-specific concerns and challenges.

Example: HubSpot's Inbound Marketing

HubSpot, a provider of inbound marketing and sales software, offers a wealth of educational content, including blog posts, e-books, webinars, and certifications. Their approach helps clients understand the value of inbound marketing and how HubSpot's tools can drive results.

Proactive Problem-Solving

Long sales cycles often involve complex problems that require innovative solutions. Sales professionals must proactively identify and address potential obstacles, demonstrating their commitment to helping clients succeed.

Example: IBM's Watson Discovery

IBM's Watson Discovery is an AI-powered platform that assists in uncovering insights from unstructured data. IBM sales professionals work closely with clients to understand their data-related challenges and proactively propose solutions, positioning Watson Discovery as a problem-solving tool.

Milestone-Based Agreements

Breaking the extended sales cycle into manageable milestones can instill confidence in clients. Sales professionals can negotiate agreements that provide clients with value at various points throughout the process.

Example: Construction Project Phases

In the construction industry, clients often enter agreements with contractors that specify payment upon reaching specific project milestones, such as completing foundation work or erecting structural elements. These milestone-based agreements provide assurance and tangible progress.

Real-Life Success Stories

Let's explore real-life success stories that illustrate the innovation and expertise required to manage long sales cycles effectively:

Example: Boeing's Aircraft Sales to Airlines

Boeing's sales of commercial aircraft to airlines involve extensive sales cycles that can span years. Their sales teams cultivate enduring relationships with airline executives and provide comprehensive support, from aircraft selection to financing solutions. Boeing's ability to manage long sales cycles has contributed to its dominance in the aerospace industry.

Example: Enterprise Software Implementation

Selling enterprise software often entails lengthy sales cycles as companies evaluate and deploy solutions that impact their entire organization. Software providers like Oracle and SAP invest in understanding clients' complex needs and offer customizable solutions. They guide clients through the implementation process, ensuring a seamless transition and long-term success.

Managing long sales cycles requires an innovative and relationship-centric approach. Sales professionals must tailor their strategies to provide customized content, proactively solve problems, and break down the journey into manageable milestones. Real-life success stories, such as Boeing's aircraft sales and enterprise software implementation, highlight the significance of these strategies in handling extended sales processes. In the world of long sales cycles, innovation is the key to sustaining client relationships, addressing complex challenges, and ultimately achieving successful outcomes that drive business growth and success.

CHAPTER 10

HANDLING DIFFICULT SITUATIONS

$\mathcal{N}$avigating the intricacies of handling difficult situations is an essential skill in the dynamic world of sales and negotiations. In this chapter, we delve into the art of managing challenging circumstances where conflicts, objections, or unexpected obstacles arise and demand innovative strategies and thoughtful approaches to achieve successful resolutions. From defusing tensions to turning adversity into opportunity, we explore real-life examples and effective techniques that empower sales professionals to confidently face adversity and emerge with mutually beneficial outcomes.

Dealing with Aggressive Buyers

Aggressive buyers can pose significant challenges during sales negotiations. They may employ tactics such as intimidation, excessive demands, or constant pressure to gain advantageous terms or concessions. Handling these situations effectively requires a strategic and empathetic approach. Let's explore some innovative strategies:

Maintain Composure and Professionalism

In the face of aggression, it's essential to remain composed and professional. Responding with professionalism not only diffuses tension but also positions the sales professional as a trustworthy and reliable partner.

Example: Luxury Real Estate Sales

In the luxury real estate market, high-net-worth buyers can be demanding and assertive. Real estate agents are trained to maintain a calm and professional demeanour, even when faced with aggressive negotiations. This approach fosters trust and confidence in clients.

Active Listening and Empathy

Understanding the underlying motivations and concerns of aggressive buyers is key. Active listening and empathetic responses can help uncover the root causes of their behaviour.

Example: Automotive Sales

In the competitive automotive industry, buyers often negotiate aggressively to secure better deals. Skilled salespeople listen attentively to their demands and ask probing questions to identify their true priorities. By addressing these concerns, they can reach mutually beneficial agreements.

Set Clear Boundaries

Sales professionals should establish and communicate clear boundaries regarding what is negotiable and what is not. This prevents aggressive buyers from making unreasonable demands or taking advantage of perceived weaknesses.

Example: High-End Jewellery Sales

In the luxury jewellery market, sales associates set clear boundaries regarding discounts and pricing. They communicate the exclusivity and value of their products, which helps deter aggressive haggling.

Offer Alternatives and Solutions

Presenting alternatives and creative solutions can help diffuse aggression. By providing options that address the buyer's concerns while preserving the integrity of the deal, sales professionals can steer negotiations in a more positive direction.

Example: Technology Solution Sales

In the technology sector, buyers may aggressively push for lower prices. Sales teams often offer alternative licensing models, additional services, or extended warranties to sweeten the deal without compromising profitability.

Real-Life Success Stories

Example: Negotiating with a Demanding Client

In the world of interior design, an interior designer faced a client who was highly demanding and aggressive in negotiations. The client insisted on steep discounts and frequent changes to the design plan. The designer, while maintaining professionalism, proposed a comprehensive design package that included a detailed mood board, virtual reality walkthroughs, and regular project updates. By demonstrating the value of the comprehensive service and addressing the client's need for involvement, the designer not only closed the deal but also exceeded the client's expectations.

Example: High-Stakes Software Sales

A software sales team encountered an aggressive buyer who demanded substantial price reductions and threatened to consider a competitor's solution. In response, the sales team offered a tiered pricing structure, allowing the buyer to start with a basic package and gradually scale up as needed. This approach met the buyer's budget constraints while securing a long-term commitment. The buyer, pleased with the flexibility and innovative solution, chose to move forward with the deal.

Dealing with aggressive buyers is a challenging but manageable aspect of sales negotiations. By maintaining composure, actively listening, setting clear boundaries, and offering creative solutions, sales professionals can effectively navigate these situations. Real-life success stories in various industries, from luxury real estate to high-stakes software sales, highlight the effectiveness of these strategies in handling aggressive buyers and achieving successful outcomes. In the dynamic world of sales, innovation and empathy are key ingredients in turning potentially adversarial situations into mutually beneficial partnerships.

Negotiating in a Stalemate

Stalemates in negotiations can occur for various reasons, including conflict of interest, stubbornness, or a lack of creative solutions. When faced with such a situation, negotiators must employ innovative approaches to reinvigorate discussions:

Strategic Pause

Sometimes, stepping back and allowing a strategic pause can help break the deadlock. This pause allows both parties to reassess their positions, objectives, and the potential for collaboration.

Example: Labour Union Negotiations

In labour union negotiations, both labour and management can reach a stalemate over issues like wages and working conditions. A strategic pause, where negotiations are temporarily halted, can provide both parties with the opportunity to consult with their constituents, re-evaluate their priorities, and return to the table with a fresh perspective.

Mediation and Neutral Facilitation

Bringing in a neutral third party, such as a mediator, can help facilitate discussions and bridge gaps between parties. A skilled mediator can provide objectivity and guide negotiations toward mutually acceptable solutions.

Example: Divorce Mediation

In divorce proceedings, spouses can often reach a stalemate when it comes to property division or child custody arrangements.

A trained mediator can help the couple navigate these difficult discussions, facilitating compromise and resolution.

Creative Problem-Solving

Innovative problem-solving techniques, such as brainstorming sessions or scenario planning, can unlock new possibilities and encourage parties to explore creative solutions.

Example: Environmental Conservation Negotiations

In negotiations related to environmental conservation and land use, stakeholders may reach a stalemate over competing interests. Creative problem-solving methods, like design charrettes or collaborative land-use planning sessions, enable parties to jointly envision sustainable solutions that balance economic and environmental concerns.

Win-Win Concessions

Rather than focusing on winning or losing, negotiators can explore concessions that benefit both parties. These win-win concessions can create goodwill and pave the way for resolution.

Example: Business Partnership Dissolution

In a business partnership dissolution, parties may reach a deadlock over asset division or compensation. By identifying and offering win-win concessions, such as shared intellectual property rights or revenue-sharing agreements, the parties can dissolve the partnership amicably.

Negotiating in a stalemate requires a blend of innovation, patience, and strategic thinking. By employing strategies such as a strategic pause, mediation, creative problem-solving, and win-win concessions, negotiators can breathe new life into discussions that have reached an impasse. Real-life success stories, from the Northern Ireland peace process to the resolution of Hollywood writers' strikes, demonstrate the effectiveness of these approaches in breaking free from deadlock and achieving mutually beneficial outcomes. In the dynamic realm of negotiations, the ability to revitalize stalled discussions is a testament to the art of negotiation itself, where innovation and perseverance prevail.

Escalating to Higher Authority

Escalating negotiations to a higher authority is a calculated move that can be employed for various reasons, including breaking deadlocks, exerting pressure, or seeking executive input. When done strategically, it can be a game-changing tactic:

Strategic Deadlock Breaker

When negotiations reach a standstill due to differences or intractability at the lower levels, escalating to higher authority can disrupt the status quo and inject fresh perspectives.

Example: Union-Management Bargaining

In labour union negotiations, lower-level bargaining teams may encounter a deadlock over issues like wages or benefits. Escalating to higher authority, such as bringing in top executives, can demonstrate the organization's commitment to resolving the dispute and may lead to a breakthrough.

Pressure and Leverage

The threat of escalation can serve as a powerful tool to exert pressure on the opposing party. It signals a willingness to bring more significant resources or authority to bear on the negotiation.

Example: Supplier Negotiations

In supplier negotiations, buyers might escalate discussions when suppliers resist price concessions or contractual terms. The threat of involving senior management can incentivise suppliers to reconsider their positions and offer more favourable terms.

Seeking Executive Input

In complex negotiations or high-stakes deals, involving senior executives or decision-makers can ensure alignment with organisational goals and strategic direction.

Example: Mergers and Acquisitions

During merger and acquisition negotiations, discussions may be escalated to senior leadership to ensure alignment with the company's overall strategy. Senior executives can provide crucial insights and make decisions that have far-reaching implications.

Maintaining Face and Negotiating Room

Escalation can also be used strategically to save face or create a negotiating room. Parties may use it as a tactic to give themselves more time or create the appearance of increased commitment.

Example: Diplomatic Negotiations

In international diplomacy, negotiations between nations may reach a passe. Diplomats may escalate discussions to their respective governments, allowing time for strategic maneuvering, internal consultations, and adjustments to positions without appearing to back down.

Innovative Approaches to Escalation

In addition to traditional escalation tactics, innovative approaches can be employed to address this subject smartly and effectively:

1. Simulated Escalation

In some cases, negotiators can employ a simulated escalation, where they communicate the intention to escalate without actually doing so. This tactic can serve as a wake-up call to the opposing party and may prompt concessions.

Example: Strategic Business Negotiations

In strategic business negotiations, a party may inform the other side that they plan to escalate the matter to their senior management or board of directors. This can lead to renewed discussions and a more flexible approach from the opposing party, even if the escalation is never executed.

2. Collaborative Escalation

Rather than using escalation as a power play, negotiators can collaborate on the escalation process. This approach involves joint discussions with higher authorities to ensure that both parties' interests are considered.

Example: Joint Ventures

In joint venture negotiations, both parties may jointly present their business case to their respective executive teams. This collaborative approach can foster trust and transparency and ensure that decisions align with the joint venture's goals.

3. Expert Facilitation

Bringing in external experts or facilitators can provide a neutral perspective and help guide discussions when negotiations are escalated. These experts can offer innovative solutions and bridge gaps between parties.

Example: Environmental Impact Assessments

In negotiations related to environmental impact assessments for large infrastructure projects, both the project developer and environmental advocates may escalate discussions to involve experts in environmental science and sustainable development. These experts can offer objective assessments and innovative mitigation strategies.

Escalating negotiations to a higher authority is a tactical move that can yield remarkable results when employed strategically. Whether as a means to break a deadlock, exert pressure, seek executive input, or create a negotiating room, it is a powerful tool in a negotiator's arsenal. In addition to traditional escalation tactics, innovative approaches like simulated escalation, collaborative escalation, and expert facilitation can be employed to address this subject smartly. Real-life success stories, such as the Treaty of Versailles negotiations and complex real estate deals, highlight the effectiveness of these approaches in achieving mutually beneficial outcomes and leveraging higher authority as a catalyst for resolution. In the dynamic realm of negotiations, innovation and strategic thinking are key to turning impasses into opportunities for progress and success.

Resolving Deadlocks in a Negotiations

Deadlocks can occur in negotiations for various reasons, including conflicting interests, communication breakdowns, or stubbornness. When negotiations reach a point where progress seems impossible, it's essential to employ innovative approaches to break the deadlock:

Active Listening and Empathy

Understanding the underlying motivations and concerns of each party can be a powerful tool for resolving deadlocks. Active listening and empathetic responses can help uncover common ground and potential solutions.

Example: Labour-Management Negotiations

In labour-management negotiations, disputes over wages and working conditions can lead to deadlocks. Effective labour leaders listen attentively to their members' concerns while management seeks to understand the financial constraints of the organization. This empathetic approach can lead to compromises that break the deadlock.

Mediation and Facilitation

Bringing in a neutral third party, such as a mediator or facilitator, can help bridge gaps between parties and facilitate constructive discussions.

Example: Divorce Mediation

In divorce proceedings, couples may reach a deadlock over property division or child custody. A skilled mediator can help the couple navigate these discussions, encouraging compromise and resolution.

Brainstorming and Creative Problem-Solving

Innovation and creativity can be harnessed to break through deadlocks. Brainstorming sessions and creative problem-solving techniques can help parties explore new ideas and alternatives.

Example: Environmental Negotiations

In negotiations related to environmental conservation and land use, stakeholders may reach a deadlock over competing interests. Collaborative design charrettes or scenario planning sessions can encourage the development of innovative solutions that balance economic and environmental concerns.

Trade-Offs and Concessions

Identifying trade-offs and concessions that both parties find acceptable can be a strategic way to break a deadlock. This approach involves finding mutually beneficial compromises.

Example: Business Partnership Dissolution

In a business partnership dissolution, deadlocks can occur over asset division or compensation. Identifying trade-offs, such as shared intellectual property rights or revenue-sharing agreements, can facilitate resolution.

Innovative Approaches to Resolving Deadlocks

In addition to traditional deadlock-resolution strategies, there are innovative approaches that can address this subject in a fresh and effective manner:

1. Outside-the-Box Solutions

Sometimes, deadlocks arise because parties are trapped in conventional thinking. Encouraging the exploration of outside-the-box solutions can lead to breakthroughs.

Example: Community Land Use Planning

In community land use planning, stakeholders may reach a deadlock over zoning issues. Innovative solutions could involve mixed-use development, green infrastructure, or community land trusts, challenging traditional zoning practices and fostering compromise.

2. Structured Decision-Making Tools

Using structured decision-making tools, such as decision trees or weighted criteria matrices, can help parties objectively evaluate options and make informed choices.

Example: Project Funding Decisions

In project funding decisions, stakeholders may reach a deadlock over budget allocation. Using a structured decision-making tool that considers factors like cost, impact, and strategic alignment can guide discussions toward data-driven decisions.

3. Digital Collaboration Platforms

Modern technology offers digital collaboration platforms that facilitate negotiations, allowing parties to engage in real-time discussions and explore potential solutions.

Example: Virtual Diplomatic Negotiations

In international diplomacy, negotiations may stall due to logistical challenges. Leveraging virtual negotiation platforms can enable diplomats to engage in discussions and propose solutions without the need for physical presence, breaking geographical deadlocks.

Real-Life Success Stories

Let's explore real-life success stories that showcase innovative approaches to resolving deadlocks:

Example: Camp David Accords

The Camp David Accords in 1978 were a ground-breaking achievement in resolving a deadlock. U.S. President Jimmy Carter facilitated negotiations between Egyptian President Anwar Sadat and Israeli Prime Minister Menachem Begin. The talks reached a critical deadlock over the status of Jerusalem. President Carter proposed a creative solution: the establishment of an autonomous Palestinian entity in the West Bank and Gaza Strip. This innovative approach broke the impasse and laid the foundation for peace.

Example: Multinational Trade Agreement

In negotiations for a multinational trade agreement involving several countries, parties reached a deadlock over tariff reductions.

A facilitator introduced a digital collaboration platform that allowed negotiators to input their preferences and see the potential outcomes of various tariff reduction scenarios. This data-driven approach enabled parties to identify mutually beneficial tariff reductions, breaking the deadlock and advancing the agreement.

Resolving deadlocks in negotiations is a dynamic process that requires a combination of innovation, empathy, and strategic thinking. Whether through active listening, mediation, brainstorming, trade-offs, or outside-the-box solutions, negotiators can employ a range of strategies to break through impasses. In addition to traditional approaches, innovative methods like structured decision-making tools and digital collaboration platforms offer fresh perspectives on resolving deadlocks. Real-life success stories, such as the Camp David Accords and multinational trade agreements, highlight the effectiveness of these approaches in achieving mutually beneficial outcomes. In the intricate realm of negotiations, innovation is the key to unlocking new possibilities, fostering compromise, and turning deadlocks into opportunities for progress and success.

CHAPTER 11

POST NEGOTIATION: MAINTAINING CUSTOMER SATISFACTION

*I*n the world of sales, the journey doesn't end when the deal is signed; it's just the beginning. Welcome to the realm of "Post-Negotiation: Maintaining Customer Satisfaction," where we delve into the art of ensuring that your customers remain not just satisfied but delighted with their decision to choose your product or service. In this chapter, we'll uncover the strategies and insights to keep those relationships strong, fulfill promises made during negotiations, and turn satisfied customers into loyal advocates. Get ready to discover how nurturing customer satisfaction can lead to long-lasting success in the dynamic world of sales.

Delivering on Promises: The Keystone of Customer Satisfaction

In the ever-evolving world of sales and negotiations, one timeless principle remains unwavering—the importance of delivering on promises." This chapter is your gateway to understanding the profound impact that fulfilling commitments and assurances made during negotiations can have on building trust, customer satisfaction, and long-term relationships. We'll embark on a journey to explore the significance of keeping your word, share real-world examples of promises that have been kept, and introduce innovative solutions to ensure you become a promise-keeping virtuoso in the dynamic realm of sales.

The Art of Promise Keeping

At the heart of any successful negotiation lies the essence of promise-keeping. Whether it's delivering a product on time, meeting quality expectations, or honoring contractual agreements, promises form the foundation of trust between buyer and seller. In a world where reputations can be made or broken in an instant, mastering this art is non-negotiable:

1. Timely Deliveries and Reliability

One of the most fundamental promises in sales is delivering products or services as agreed upon—on time and with unwavering reliability. Consistently meeting deadlines and exceeding expectations can elevate customer satisfaction to new heights.

Example: E-commerce Giants

Online retailers like Amazon have built their empires on the promise of timely deliveries. Their use of advanced logistics and delivery networks not only meets customer expectations but often surpasses them, setting a gold standard in the industry.

2. Quality Assurance

Another critical promise centers around the quality of what is offered. Assuring customers that your product or service will meet or exceed their expectations can lead to lasting satisfaction and loyalty.

Example: Luxury Automobile Manufacturers

Luxury automobile manufacturers like BMW or Mercedes-Benz promise superior quality and craftsmanship. The meticulous attention to detail and rigorous quality control processes they adhere to ensure that they consistently deliver on this promise.

3. Transparent Communication

Open and honest communication is a promise in itself. Keeping customers informed about any changes, delays, or challenges along the way fosters trust and demonstrates your commitment to their satisfaction.

Example: Airlines

In the airline industry, where unforeseen disruptions like weather delays are common, carriers often communicate proactively with passengers. They provide timely updates, alternatives, and compensation when necessary, all of which contribute to maintaining customer satisfaction despite challenges.

Innovative Solutions for Keeping Promise

In addition to traditional promise-keeping practices, innovative solutions can help you go above and beyond in delivering on your commitments:

1. Predictive Analytics

Leveraging predictive analytics can enable you to anticipate and proactively address potential challenges in delivering on promises. By analysing historical data and market trends, you can optimize your processes and minimize disruptions.

Example: Food Delivery Services

Food delivery services use predictive analytics to estimate delivery times more accurately. By factoring in variables like traffic, weather, and order preparation times, they provide customers with realistic delivery windows, reducing frustration and enhancing satisfaction.

2. Customer Feedback Loop

Creating a feedback loop with your customers can help you continuously improve your promise-keeping capabilities. Soliciting feedback and acting on it not only resolves issues promptly but also demonstrates your commitment to their satisfaction.

Example: Online Retailers

E-commerce giants often seek customer feedback after every purchase. They use this data not only to address individual concerns but also to make systemic improvements in their supply chains, packaging, and delivery processes.

3. Technology-Driven Transparency

Leveraging technology, such as real-time tracking and automated notifications, can provide customers with unprecedented transparency into the status of their orders or projects. This level of visibility enhances their confidence in your ability to deliver on promises.

Example: Ride-Sharing Apps

Ride-sharing apps like Uber and Lyft use real-time tracking and updates to keep passengers informed about the location of their drivers and estimated arrival times. This technology-driven transparency has become a hallmark of the industry.

Real-Life Success Stories

Let's delve into real-life success stories that highlight the power of delivering on promises:

Example: FedEx's "Absolutely, Positively" slogan

FedEx's iconic slogan, "When it absolutely, positively has to be there overnight," underscores the company's commitment to timely deliveries. This promise-keeping ethos has made FedEx a global leader in the logistics industry.

The art of delivering on promises stands as a cornerstone of building trust and customer satisfaction. Whether it's through timely deliveries, quality assurance, or transparent communication, fulfilling commitments remains the key to success. Moreover, innovative solutions like predictive analytics, customer feedback loops, and technology-driven transparency allow you to not only meet but exceed customer expectations. Real-life success stories, from SpaceX's reusable rockets to FedEx's iconic slogan, exemplify the profound impact of promise-keeping. As you embark on your journey in sales, remember that each promise fulfilled not only builds customer satisfaction but also solidifies your reputation as a trusted partner in the pursuit of mutually beneficial outcomes.

Managing Expectations: The Art of Surpassing What's Promised

In the dynamic world of sales and negotiations, one skill stands out as essential for building lasting trust and satisfaction—managing expectations. This chapter is your gateway to understanding how skill-fully aligning and exceeding what's promised can elevate customer satisfaction, nurture relationships, and foster loyalty. We'll embark on a journey to explore the profound significance of expectation management, share real-world examples of exemplary practices, and introduce innovative solutions to ensure you become an expert in this art within the dynamic realm of sales.

The Significance of Expectation Management

Expectations play a pivotal role in the world of sales and negotiations. They are the lens through which customers perceive and evaluate the value of your product or service. Skillful management of these expectations can make the difference between a satisfied customer and a delighted advocate:

1. Setting Realistic Baselines

One of the foundational aspects of managing expectations is setting realistic baselines. It involves making promises that you are confident you can deliver on consistently. This prevents overpromising, which can lead to disappointment.

Example: Smartphone Manufacturers

Smartphone manufacturers often set realistic baselines by promising specific features and specifications for their devices. By consistently delivering on these promises, they maintain customer trust and satisfaction.

2. Under-promising and Overdelivering

A time-tested strategy for managing expectations is under-promising and overdelivering. It involves setting modest expectations and then surpassing them, which can lead to pleasantly surprised customers.

Example: Fast Food Chains

Fast food chains frequently employ this strategy with delivery times. They might estimate a delivery time of 30 minutes but consistently deliver in 20 minutes or less. Customers experience the delight of receiving their orders earlier than expected.

3. Transparent Communication

Open and transparent communication is another cornerstone of expectation management. Keeping customers informed about potential delays, challenges, or changes in circumstances fosters trust and demonstrates your commitment to their satisfaction.

Example: Package Delivery Services

Package delivery services communicate transparently with customers about delivery status. They provide real-time tracking information and notify customers about any unexpected delays. This level of transparency enhances customer confidence.

Innovative Solutions for Expectation Management

Beyond traditional practices, innovative solutions can enhance your ability to manage expectations effectively:

1. AI-Powered Predictive Insights

Leveraging AI and predictive analytics can help you anticipate customer needs and behaviours. These insights enable you to proactively manage expectations and provide personalized experiences.

Example: E-commerce Platforms

E-commerce platforms use AI to analyse customer behaviour and make product recommendations. By showing customers products they are likely to be interested in, these platforms manage and even exceed expectations by creating a tailored shopping experience.

2. Interactive Customer Portals

Interactive customer portals offer customers real-time visibility into their orders, projects, or accounts. These portals empower customers to manage their expectations actively.

Example: Banking Apps

Banking apps provide customers with real-time access to their account balances, transaction history, and upcoming payments. This transparency helps customers manage their financial expectations and make informed decisions.

3. Service-Level Agreements (SLAs)

In B2B negotiations, service-level agreements (SLAs) are contractual commitments that define specific performance expectations. Implementing SLAs can formalize and manage expectations for both parties.

Example: IT Service Providers

IT service providers often enter into SLAs with their clients, specifying response times for resolving technical issues. These agreements set clear expectations for service quality and response times.

Real-Life Success Stories

Let's delve into real-life success stories that underscore the power of managing expectations:

Example: Disney's Magic-Band System

Disney's Magic-Band system is a prime example of expectation management in the entertainment industry. By providing guests with wearable technology that allows access to attractions, reservations, and more, Disney sets high expectations for a seamless and magical experience. The system not only meets these expectations but often exceeds them, creating memorable and delighted visitors.

Example: Online Streaming Services

Online streaming services like Netflix and Amazon Prime Video manage expectations effectively through personalized recommendations and content curation. By using algorithms to predict what users might enjoy, these platforms often surprise users with content that surpasses their initial expectations.

In the dynamic world of sales and negotiations, the art of managing expectations stands as a linchpin of building trust and customer satisfaction. By setting realistic baselines, under-promising and overdelivering, and communicating transparently, you can elevate customer perceptions and foster loyalty. Moreover, innovative solutions like AI-powered predictive insights, interactive customer portals, and SLAs empower you to not only meet but exceed customer expectations. Real-life success stories, from Disney's Magic-Band system to online streaming services, exemplify the transformative impact of expectation management. As you embark on your journey in sales, remember that managing expectations is the key to nurturing relationships and turning satisfied customers into loyal advocates, driving long-term success and growth.

Strategies to Avoid Post-Sale Disputes: Nurturing Smooth Sailing

In the intricate world of sales and negotiations, where promises are made and deals are sealed, the quest for harmony doesn't end with the dotted line. Welcome to the realm of avoiding post-sale disputes, where we embark on a journey to understand the proactive measures you can take to sidestep conflicts altogether. This chapter serves as your guide to maintaining tranquility in the aftermath of a deal, offering real-world examples of dispute prevention and introducing innovative solutions to help you become a master of harmony in the dynamic arena of sales.

The Value of Proactive Dispute Avoidance

While disputes may seem like an inherent part of the business landscape, the truth is that many of them can be avoided altogether. By taking proactive measures to manage expectations, enhance communication, and build trust, you can significantly reduce the likelihood of conflicts:

1. Clear and Comprehensive Contracts

One of the cornerstones of dispute avoidance is crafting clear and comprehensive contracts. These agreements should leave no room for ambiguity, clearly defining the terms, responsibilities, and expectations of all parties involved.

Example: Construction Contracts

In the construction industry, detailed contracts specifying project scope, timelines, materials, and payment terms can prevent disputes by providing a solid foundation for the project.

2. Regular Communication

Open and regular communication is key to preventing misunderstandings and mistrust. Maintaining an ongoing dialogue with clients can help you address issues before they escalate into disputes.

Example: Software Development

Software development firms often hold regular status meetings with clients to discuss progress, challenges, and changes in project scope. This ongoing communication minimizes the risk of misunderstandings.

3. Educate and Set Realistic Expectations

Educating clients about the intricacies of your products or services and setting realistic expectations can prevent disputes stemming from unrealistic assumptions.

Example: Financial Planning Services

Financial planners often educate clients about the potential risks and returns associated with investments. Setting realistic expectations about investment performance can prevent disputes when markets fluctuate.

Innovative Solutions for Dispute Avoidance

In addition to traditional practices, innovative solutions can elevate your dispute avoidance game:

1. AI-Powered Risk Assessment

Leveraging AI for risk assessment can help you identify potential issues early in the sales process. By analysing historical data and customer behaviours, AI can flag high-risk deals for closer scrutiny.

Example: Insurance Underwriting

Insurance companies use AI algorithms to assess the risk associated with each policy. By identifying high-risk customers or policyholders, they can adjust premiums or coverage to mitigate potential disputes.

2. Customer Self-Service Portals

Empowering customers with self-service portals allows them to manage their accounts, orders, or services independently. These portals can reduce errors, enhance communication, and provide real-time access to information.

Example: Telecommunications Providers

Telecommunications companies often offer customer self-service portals where users can check their bills, update contact information, and troubleshoot common issues without the need for customer support interactions.

Real-Life Success Stories

Let's explore real-life success stories that illustrate the power of proactive dispute avoidance:

Example: Amazon's Return Policy

Amazon's customer-centric return policy, which allows customers to return products easily, serves as a model for dispute avoidance. By making returns hassle-free, Amazon reduces disputes and enhances customer trust.

Avoiding post-sale disputes is a proactive approach to preserving harmony and trust. By crafting clear contracts, maintaining open communication, and setting realistic expectations, you can significantly reduce the risk of conflicts. Innovative solutions such as blockchain for transparency, AI-powered risk assessment, and customer self-service portals offer modern ways to enhance your dispute avoidance efforts. Real-life success stories, from Amazon's return policy to legal consultancies' practices, underscore the transformative impact of proactive dispute avoidance. As you navigate the intricate landscape of sales, remember that disputes are not inevitable; they are challenges that can be pre-emptively addressed through diligence, communication, and innovation.

Building Customer Loyalty: The Art of Cultivating Unbreakable Bonds

In the ever-evolving world of sales and negotiations, where transactions are made and relationships are forged, there exists a treasure trove of value beyond the initial deal—the treasure known as "customer loyalty." In this segment, we embark on a journey to unlock the secrets of nurturing long-lasting customer relationships that transcend individual transactions. We'll explore the profound significance of customer loyalty, share real-world examples of loyalty-building practices, and introduce innovative solutions to help you become a maestro in the dynamic realm of sales.

The Invaluable Essence of Customer Loyalty

Customer loyalty is not merely a buzzword; it's the lifeblood of any successful business. It's the golden thread that weaves together sustained growth, enhanced reputation, and enduring profitability. Here's why it matters:

1. Repeat Business

Loyal customers are more likely to return for repeat purchases. They become a consistent source of revenue, reducing the need for constant acquisition efforts.

Example: Coffee Chains

Coffee chains like Starbucks thrive on customer loyalty. Regular customers often visit daily or weekly, contributing significantly to the company's revenue.

2. Referrals and Advocacy

Loyal customers aren't just satisfied; they're your best advocates. They refer friends, family, and colleagues, amplifying your customer base at no additional cost.

Example: Tech Gadgets

Tech enthusiasts who are loyal to specific brands often influence others through word-of-mouth recommendations, social media, or online forums.

3. Resistance to Competitive Offers

Loyal customers are less likely to switch to competitors, even when presented with tempting offers or lower prices. Their loyalty acts as a protective shield for your business.

Example: Mobile Phone Providers

Mobile phone providers often rely on loyalty programs and exclusive perks to retain customers in a highly competitive market.

Innovative Solutions for Building Customer Loyalty

Beyond traditional methods, innovative solutions can help you build and fortify customer loyalty:

1. Personalized Customer Experiences

Leveraging data and technology, you can offer personalized experiences that cater to individual preferences. Personalization goes beyond addressing customers by their first name—it's about understanding their needs and offering tailored solutions.

Example: E-commerce Platforms

E-commerce giants like Amazon use algorithms to recommend products based on a customer's browsing and purchase history, creating a highly personalized shopping experience.

2. Loyalty Programs with a Twist

Rethink traditional loyalty programs by introducing gamification, surprise rewards, or tiered systems. Engaging customers in a fun and rewarding journey can strengthen their loyalty.

Example: Airlines

Airlines often employ tiered loyalty programs that offer increasing benefits as customers accumulate more miles or segments flown. This system encourages travellers to stick with the same airline for the promise of better rewards.

3. Exceptional Customer Support

Providing exceptional customer support can set you apart from competitors. Offer various channels for support, quick response times, and knowledgeable representatives who can resolve issues promptly.

Example: Online Retailers

Online retailers like Zappos are known for their exceptional customer support. They empower their representatives to go above and beyond to satisfy customers, even if it means accepting returns with no questions asked.

Real-Life Success Stories

Let's delve into real-life success stories that exemplify the power of building customer loyalty:

Example: Apple's Ecosystem

Apple has created a loyal customer base by developing an ecosystem of products and services that seamlessly integrate. Customers who invest in one Apple product often become loyal to the brand and purchase additional Apple devices and services.

Example: Disney's Magical Experience

Disney theme parks are renowned for providing a magical experience that fosters customer loyalty. Visitors often return to relive the enchantment and bring their families, creating a multi-generational tradition of loyalty.

Building customer loyalty is the key to unlocking long-term success and profitability. Loyal customers are the lifeblood of your business, offering repeat business, referrals, and resistance to competitive offers. Innovative solutions such as personalized customer experiences, revamped loyalty programs, and exceptional customer support can elevate your loyalty-building efforts. Real-life success stories, from Apple's ecosystem to Disney's magical experience, underscore the transformative power of customer loyalty. As you navigate the intricate landscape of sales, remember that building customer loyalty is not a one-time transaction; it's a journey of trust, care, and exceeding expectations, leading to enduring relationships and prosperity.

CHAPTER 12

CONTINUOUS IMPROVEMENT IN SALES NEGOTIATION

*E*mbarking on the path of excellence in sales negotiation is a journey with no final destination—instead, it's a continuous voyage of growth and refinement. In this chapter, we explore the art of perpetual enhancement and evolution in the dynamic arena of sales. In this chapter, we'll delve into the pivotal role of ongoing improvement, share real-world examples of businesses that have thrived through this philosophy, and introduce innovative solutions to empower you on your quest for excellence. So, fasten your seatbelts as we set sail on the ever-changing seas of sales negotiation improvement!

The Role of Feedback in Sales Negotiation: Navigating Success

In the dynamic world of sales and negotiations, where relationships are cultivated and deals sealed, there's a crucial element that often goes underappreciated—the power of "feedback." Feedback isn't just a construct of business etiquette; it's the compass that guides us toward continuous improvement and unparalleled success in the intricate dance of sales negotiation. This part of the segment explores the pivotal role that feedback plays, not only in enhancing our skills but also in fortifying customer relationships. We'll delve into the significance of feedback, offer actionable ideas for soliciting and utilizing feedback effectively, and showcase real-world examples of how feedback can propel businesses to new heights.

The Essence of Feedback in Sales Negotiation

Feedback is the process of gathering information about your performance and making adjustments based on that information. In sales negotiation, feedback serves a multitude of purposes, each contributing to your growth and success:

1. Self-Reflection and Improvement

Feedback is like a mirror that reflects your strengths and areas for improvement. It helps you identify what you're doing right and where you can enhance your skills.

Example: Sales Calls

After a sales call, you might receive feedback from a colleague or manager about your presentation style. This feedback can lead to refinements in your approach, ultimately improving your sales pitch.

2. Customer-Centric Approach

Feedback from customers is a precious resource for tailoring your offerings to their needs and preferences. It allows you to align your solutions more closely with their expectations.

Example: Product Development

Tech companies often gather user feedback to enhance their products. Customer suggestions and pain points inform updates and features that cater to their specific requirements.

3. Relationship Building

Soliciting feedback demonstrates your commitment to customer satisfaction and shows that you value their opinions. This can foster trust and stronger, long-lasting relationships.

Example: Account Management

Account managers often conduct regular feedback sessions with clients to gauge satisfaction levels, address concerns, and build rapport. This proactive approach strengthens client relationships.

Strategies for Effective Feedback Solicitation

To leverage the power of feedback, you need strategies for soliciting it effectively:

1. Create Safe Spaces

Encourage open and honest feedback by creating a safe and non-judgmental environment. Assure your counterparts that their opinions are valued and will be used constructively.

2. Asking the Right Questions

Frame your feedback requests with specific questions that elicit actionable responses. Instead of asking, "Do you have any feedback?" ask, "What aspects of our proposal could be improved to better meet your needs?"

3. Timing Is Key

Request feedback at appropriate times in the negotiation process. You might seek initial impressions after a presentation and follow up with a more comprehensive request once the deal is concluded.

4. Diversify Your Sources

Don't limit feedback to a single perspective. Seek input from colleagues, managers, clients, and even competitors to gain a well-rounded view of your performance.

5. Leverage Technology

Utilize tools and platforms that facilitate feedback collection, such as online surveys, feedback forms, or automated follow-up emails.

Actionable Ideas for Feedback Utilization

Feedback is valuable only when put into action. Here are some actionable ideas to make the most of the feedback you receive:

1. Develop Personalized Improvement Plans

Use feedback to create personalized improvement plans. Identify specific areas where you can enhance your skills and set clear goals for growth.

Example: Skills Matrix

Create a skills matrix based on feedback and self-assessment. Regularly track your progress and adjust your development plan accordingly.

2. Communicate Your Commitment

After receiving feedback, communicate your commitment to improvement to your counterparts. Let them know the steps you're taking to address their suggestions.

Example: Improvement Updates

Send periodic updates to clients or colleagues detailing the actions you've taken in response to their feedback. This demonstrates your dedication to their satisfaction.

3. Share Success Stories

Highlight instances where feedback led to positive outcomes. Share success stories that showcase how feedback-driven changes have benefited your customers and your organization.

Example: Feedback Corner

Create a dedicated section on your website or in your marketing materials to showcase customer success stories attributed to feedback-driven improvements.

Real-Life Success Stories

Let's explore real-life success stories that underscore the transformative power of feedback:

Example: Airbnb's Host Feedback

Airbnb empowers hosts to provide feedback on guests and vice versa. This two-way feedback system fosters trust and encourages both hosts and guests to improve their behaviours.

Example: Sales Training Programs

Sales training programs often incorporate feedback from salespeople and clients to continually enhance their curriculum. This iterative approach results in more effective training.

In the intricate landscape of sales negotiation, feedback is your compass, guiding you toward continual improvement, customer-centric solutions, and stronger relationships. By recognizing the essence of feedback, employing effective solicitation strategies, and taking actionable steps to utilize feedback, you can harness its transformative power. Real-life success stories, from Airbnb's feedback system to iterative sales training programs, highlight the profound impact that feedback can have on businesses. As you navigate the dynamic seas of sales negotiation, remember that feedback isn't just information; it's the wind in your sails, propelling you toward unparalleled success and enduring customer satisfaction.

Learning from Each Negotiation: Unveiling the Treasures Within

In the riveting world of sales negotiation, where deals are crafted, and alliances are formed, there exists an invaluable resource often overlooked—a treasure trove of wisdom that resides in every negotiation. In this segment, we embark on a journey to unearth the gems hidden within every deal. Here, we delve into the profound importance of gleaning insights from each negotiation, offer practical strategies for extracting actionable lessons, and showcase real-world examples of how embracing this philosophy can lead to exponential growth and mastery in the realm of sales.

#The Wisdom in Every Negotiation

Each negotiation, whether successful or challenging, carries within it the seeds of wisdom. Here's why it's crucial to recognize the wealth of knowledge embedded in every interaction:

1. Personal Growth and Mastery

Every negotiation presents an opportunity for personal growth and skill refinement. By reflecting on your experiences, you can continuously enhance your negotiation prowess.

Example: Sales Pitches

Sales professionals often improve their pitch strategies by analyzing past negotiations. They refine their approaches, adapt to different customer types, and refine their messaging.

2. Building Adaptive Strategies

No two negotiations are identical. By learning from each unique encounter, you develop the ability to adapt your strategies to various situations and personalities.

Example: Real Estate

Real estate agents adapt their negotiation tactics based on factors like market conditions, client preferences, and property types. This adaptability increases their effectiveness.

3. Enhancing Relationship Building

Negotiations provide insights into the art of relationship building. Understanding the dynamics of each negotiation helps you cultivate stronger and more enduring partnerships.

Example: Key Account Management

Key account managers build trust by understanding each client's preferences, communication style, and pain points through past negotiations.

Strategies for Effective Learning

To unlock the lessons within each negotiation, you need effective strategies for reflection and analysis:

1. Post-Negotiation Debriefs

Conduct post-negotiation debriefs to analyse what went well and what could be improved. This collaborative exercise can provide valuable perspectives.

Example: Two-Question Debrief

Ask two simple questions after each negotiation: "What worked?" and "What could we do differently next time?" This concise format encourages reflection.

2. Journaling

Maintain a negotiation journal where you record your thoughts, observations, and key takeaways after each negotiation. Regular journaling can help you identify patterns and trends.

Example: Reflective Prompts

Use reflective prompts like "What surprised me in this negotiation?" or "What would I do differently if I could redo this negotiation?" to guide your journal entries.

3. Seek Feedback

Request feedback from colleagues, mentors, or even counterparts in the negotiation. External perspectives can provide insights you might have missed.

Example: 360-Degree Feedback

Gather feedback from various sources involved in the negotiation, including colleagues, supervisors, and clients. This comprehensive approach offers diverse insights.

Actionable Lessons for Continuous Growth

The wisdom extracted from each negotiation becomes a stepping stone for your growth:

1. Identify Patterns

Review your past negotiations to identify recurring patterns. Recognizing patterns helps you anticipate challenges and adjust your strategies accordingly.

Example: Pattern Recognition Matrix

Create a matrix that categorizes different negotiation scenarios and the strategies that proved effective in each case. Use this as a reference guide.

2. Develop Playbooks

Based on your lessons learned, develop negotiation playbooks that outline effective approaches and responses to common situations.

Example: Playbook Library

Organize your negotiation playbooks by scenario or client type. This library of playbooks becomes a valuable resource for your negotiations.

3. Share Insights

Share your insights and lessons with colleagues and team members. Fostering a culture of learning within your organization can lead to collective growth.

Example: Weekly Insights

Share one key insight or lesson from your negotiations with your team every week. Encourage others to do the same to create a culture of continuous learning.

#Real-Life Success Stories

Let's explore real-life success stories that illustrate the transformative power of learning from each negotiation:

Example: Automobile Sales

Automobile sales professionals continuously refine their negotiation strategies by learning from each interaction. They adapt to evolving customer expectations, economic conditions, and market trends.

Example: Technology Solutions

Technology solution providers use insights from past negotiations to develop customized offerings for clients. Learning from each negotiation allows them to deliver tailored solutions.

Every interaction holds the potential for growth and mastery. By recognizing the wisdom within each negotiation, employing effective reflection strategies, and embracing actionable lessons, you can continuously enhance your negotiation skills. Real-life success stories, from automobile sales to technology solutions, showcase the transformative power of learning from each negotiation. As you navigate the intricate landscape of sales, remember that each negotiation is not just a transaction; it's a lesson waiting to be learned, a source of growth, and a stepping stone toward mastery in the art of negotiation.

Developing Your Negotiation Skills: Unveiling the Path to Excellence

The journey to mastery is an ongoing adventure—a quest to refine your skills, deepen your understanding, and continually evolve as a negotiator. In this chapter, we delve into the significance of skill development, offer actionable strategies for enhancing your negotiation prowess, and provide real-world examples that illustrate the transformative power of continuous learning.

The Essence of Developing Your Skills

Negotiation skills are the foundation upon which successful sales transactions and lasting relationships are built. Here's why developing your negotiation skills is pivotal:

1. Competitive Advantage

Effective negotiation skills give you a competitive edge. In a world where differentiation is key, the ability to negotiate adeptly sets you apart from the competition.

Example: Real Estate

In the competitive real estate market, agents with superior negotiation skills can secure better deals for their clients, making them highly sought after.

2. Value Creation

Negotiation isn't just about getting the best deal for yourself; it's about creating value for all parties involved. Developing your skills allows you to craft win-win solutions that foster long-term partnerships.

Example: Vendor Relationships

Procurement professionals who excel in negotiation often create mutually beneficial agreements with vendors, leading to cost savings and collaborative innovation.

3. Adaptability

The negotiation landscape is ever-changing. Developing your skills equips you with the adaptability to navigate diverse scenarios, from complex B2B deals to customer-centric sales.

Example: Pharmaceutical Sales

Pharmaceutical sales representatives continually develop their negotiation skills to adapt to evolving healthcare regulations, market dynamics, and customer expectations.

Strategies for Skill Development

To embark on the journey of skill development, consider the following strategies:

1. Training and Workshops

Participate in negotiation training programs and workshops that provide structured learning and hands-on practice.

Example: Negotiation Simulations

Engage in negotiation simulations to hone your skills in a risk-free environment. Simulations replicate real-world scenarios, allowing you to experiment with different strategies.

2. Self-Assessment

Regularly assess your negotiation skills and identify areas for improvement. Self-awareness is the first step toward growth.

Example: Skill Evaluation Framework

Create a skill evaluation framework that assesses your strengths and weaknesses in negotiation. Use this as a roadmap for development.

3. Mentorship

Seek mentorship from seasoned negotiators who can provide guidance, share insights, and offer feedback.

Example: Reverse Mentorship

Consider reverse mentorship, where younger colleagues with expertise in advanced negotiation techniques or emerging trends mentor more experienced negotiators.

#Real-Life Success Stories

Let's explore real-life success stories that exemplify the transformative power of developing negotiation skills:

Example: International Diplomacy

Skilled diplomats continuously develop their negotiation abilities to navigate complex geopolitical issues. Their expertise in negotiation has led to peace agreements and diplomatic breakthroughs.

Example: Global Sales Teams

Global sales teams invest in cross-cultural negotiation training to understand the nuances of international markets. This skill development results in successful global expansion.

In the dynamic arena of sales and negotiations, developing your negotiation skills is the compass that guides you toward excellence. Whether you seek a competitive advantage, aspire to create value, or aim to adapt to diverse negotiation scenarios, skill development is the path to mastery. Real-life success stories, from international diplomacy to global sales teams, showcase the transformative power of continuous learning. As you embark on your journey to enhance your negotiation skills, remember that it's not just a quest for personal growth; it's an investment in your success as a negotiator and a testament to your commitment to delivering exceptional value to those you serve.

Staying Updated with Industry Trends: Navigating the Shifting Tides

In the ever-evolving landscape of sales and negotiations, success hinges on your ability to not just keep pace with industry trends but to lead the charge. In this segment, we embark on a journey to uncover the profound importance of staying ahead of the curve. Here, we delve into why staying updated with industry trends is pivotal, provide actionable strategies for staying informed, and offer real-world examples that illustrate the transformative power of industry knowledge.

The Significance of Industry Trends

Staying updated with industry trends is akin to having a GPS in the dynamic landscape of sales negotiation. Here's why it's crucial:

1. Informed Decision-Making

Industry trends offer insights into customer preferences, market dynamics, and emerging technologies. This knowledge empowers you to make informed decisions.

Example: E-commerce

E-commerce businesses leverage trend data to optimize their online platforms, creating seamless and personalized shopping experiences for customers.

2. Competitive Edge

Being aware of industry trends gives you a competitive edge. You can anticipate shifts in customer demands and adapt your strategies accordingly.

Example: Retail

Retailers who embraced e-commerce early in response to industry trends gained a significant advantage over those who lagged behind.

3. Innovation Catalyst

Industry trends often herald innovative solutions. Staying updated allows you to harness these innovations to improve your negotiation techniques.

Example: Artificial Intelligence

Sales professionals incorporate AI-driven tools to analyse customer data, predict preferences, and personalize their offers based on industry trends.

Strategies for Staying Informed

To stay ahead in the game, consider these strategies:

1. Industry Publications

Subscribe to industry-specific publications, journals, and magazines. These sources provide in-depth analysis and expert opinions on the latest trends.

Example: Trend Tracking Spreadsheet

Create a spreadsheet to track trends over time. Note their emergence, growth, and potential impact on your industry.

2. Webinars and Conferences

Attend webinars, conferences, and trade shows related to your field. These events offer networking opportunities and access to thought leaders.

Example: Trend Workshops

Host internal trend workshops within your organization. Encourage team members to share insights from industry events they've attended.

3. Online Communities

Join online forums, LinkedIn groups, and social media communities dedicated to your industry. Engaging with peers can provide real-time updates on trends.

Example: Trend Discussion Forum

Create a dedicated forum within your organization to discuss industry trends. Encourage team members to contribute articles and insights they come across.

Real-Life Success Stories

Let's explore real-life success stories that exemplify the transformative power of staying updated with industry trends:

Example: Technology Start-ups

Start-ups in the technology sector continually monitor industry trends to identify gaps in the market. Their ability to spot emerging opportunities has led to disruptive innovations.

Example: Financial Services

Financial institutions leverage real-time market data and AI-driven trend analysis to make data-informed investment decisions. This approach enhances their portfolio performance.

In the domain of sales negotiation, staying updated with industry trends is your compass, guiding you toward informed decisions, a competitive edge, and innovative solutions. Whether you seek to make data-informed decisions, gain a competitive edge, or catalyse innovation, industry knowledge is your most potent asset. Real-life success stories, from technology start-ups to financial services, underscore the transformative power of staying informed. As you embark on your journey to navigate industry trends, remember that it's not just about keeping up; it's about seizing opportunities, leading the way, and ensuring your success as a forward-thinking negotiator.

CONCLUSION

A Journey to Mastery: Conclusion

As we draw the curtains on our journey through the art of sales negotiation, it's time to reflect on the key takeaways, offer encouragement for ongoing improvement, and leave you with a parting thought on becoming a masterful sales negotiator.

Recap of Key Takeaways

Throughout this book, we've explored the intricate dance of sales negotiation, uncovering its many facets and intricacies. Here's a brief recap of the key takeaways:

1. Understanding the Basics: We began by defining sales negotiation and its various stages, from prospecting to closing the deal.
2. Building Rapport and Trust: We explored the paramount importance of trust, credibility, and effective communication in building lasting relationships.
3. Negotiation Strategies: We delved into a range of negotiation strategies, from win-win vs. win-lose approaches to principled negotiation and creating value.

4. Handling Objections and Pushback: We equipped you with the tools to navigate objections effectively, turning them into opportunities for agreement.
5. Continuous Improvement: We emphasized the importance of continuous learning and self-assessment, recognizing that each negotiation is a source of valuable lessons.
6. Staying Updated with Industry Trends: We highlighted the significance of staying informed about industry trends to make informed decisions and gain a competitive edge.

Encouragement for Ongoing Improvement

The journey to mastery is never truly complete. It's a path of continual growth and refinement. We encourage you to embrace the following principles on your journey to becoming a masterful sales negotiator:

1. Embrace Learning: Never stop learning. Seek out new ideas, strategies, and insights. The world of sales negotiation is dynamic, and staying current is essential.
2. Practice Self-Reflection: Regularly assess your negotiation skills and seek feedback from peers, mentors, and clients. Self-awareness is the cornerstone of improvement.
3. Adaptability: Be open to change and adaptable to evolving trends and technologies. Embracing innovation can give you a significant advantage.
4. Share Knowledge: Share your insights and knowledge with others. Mentorship and collaboration can accelerate your growth and benefit your industry as a whole.

5. Persevere: Remember that mastery takes time. There will be challenges and setbacks along the way, but persistence is the key to success.

Parting Thought on Becoming a Masterful Sales Negotiator

As you continue your journey in the world of sales negotiation, remember this: Becoming a masterful negotiator is not just about closing deals; it's about creating value, building relationships, and leaving a lasting impact. It's about understanding the needs of others and finding solutions that benefit all parties involved. It's about being a trusted advisor, a skilled communicator, and a lifelong learner.

In the end, the art of sales negotiation is not just a business skill; it's a life skill. It's about navigating the complexities of human interaction with grace and finesse. It's about achieving success while upholding the principles of honesty, integrity, and respect.

So, as you step forward on your path to mastery, do so with enthusiasm, curiosity, and a commitment to excellence. Embrace each negotiation as an opportunity to learn, grow, and make a positive impact. And always remember that the journey itself is the destination—the journey to becoming a masterful sales negotiator is a journey to becoming the best version of yourself. I wish you luck for your bright future as a successful negotiator!

www.ingramcontent.com/pod-product-compliance
Lightning Source LLC
LaVergne TN
LVHW061544070526
838199LV00077B/6892